"This book gives power ⁙⁙⁙ ʼeate the life you want. You w⁙⁙⁙ and starts, the sense of moving forward and the temptation to go back... be prepared to be highly rewarded for taking time to pause, reflect and turn inward!"

~ Heather Clarke, Executive Coach and fellow traveler | www.hccoach.ca

"As I journeyed through this book and completed the journal exercises, I changed how I felt about myself inside out, which is why I highly recommend you read this book. It is written from the heart of a woman who has journeyed between places and arrived safely and whole. Paula Anstett asks that you, "be willing to look at all of your feelings in a new light." I did, and I am happy I journeyed through her book."

~ Wendy McIsaac, B.A., B. Ed., M. Ed.

"Heart-opening, mind-blowing, and an invite to journey within and connect with yourself, this book will help you gain clarity and propel forward with a renewed perspective. A must-read no matter the life stage you are at. Get ready to take some massive, messy, yet inspired action!"

~ Tania Moraes-Vaz, Editor / Coauthor "Dear Stress, I'm Breaking Up With You" & "On Her Plate"

"People don't love when we change. When I chose a different path, this book helped me communicate well with people, and to trust that I know what is best for ME. We are here to share our life, not lose ourself by trying to satisfy everyone else."

~ Ky-Lee Hanson, Publisher / Author / Bosswoman at Golden Brick Road Publishing House

The Journey Between Places

And Exploring What Shows Up Along The Way

The Journey Between Places

And Exploring What Shows Up Along The Way

Paula Anstett

Published in Canada, for Global Distribution by Golden Brick Road Publishing House Inc.
www.goldenbrickroad.pub
For more information email: paulaanstett@rogers.com
www.paulaanstett.com
ISBN
trade paperback: 978-1-988736-29-7
ebook: 978-1-988736-33-4
kindle: 978-1-988736-34-1
To order additional copies of this book: orders@gbrph.ca

Contents

Dedication

I dedicate this book to the intuition within each of us.
Let your intuition, not fear, be your trusted guide.

~ Paula

Preface

"Just for today, I will have the courage I need to listen to, and act upon, what I need and desire, without fear, without judgment."
~ Paula Anstett

The Journey Between Places was written to help bring awareness to the place in between, what it is, what shows up when traveling through it, and the feelings that come and the permission to be in it. To encourage you to explore your current relationship with your intuition and recognize the importance of reconnecting with it and listening to it. To help develop a relationship with your intuition that includes trust and honor.

My book is not based on science, but rather reflects my own experiences, insights, and observations that I have noticed as I walked my path, and have been witness to the spaces I watched others move through. For me, the place in between is a space we journey through during times of momentous change; the type of change that creates crisis, chaos and can cause us to question almost everything we know. Such change can occur in various areas of our lives such as relationships, health, career, finances, parenting, personal goals and aspirations. These areas are interconnected, hence when one area of our life is affected, a domino effect follows into all areas.

Often, we feel things within, and because it is a feeling, it can defy words and logic, leaving us unable to make sense of it. In an attempt to understand these feelings, it is common to talk to friends, partners, family and maybe even others in our community with the hope that they can help interpret what we are feeling. It can cause us to feel even more confused and sometimes, even feel guilty for feeling a certain way in the first place. Who do we listen to? Who has the answer? The voice that lies deep within has the answer. It is our personal, no glitch GPS system. Can you hear it? Do you trust it?

We are born with this flawless internal GPS system whose role is to be our ever-trusted friend, confidant, and someone who knows the way. Though our intuition never leaves us, after years of being silenced and ignored, it is often hard to hear. It is as though it lies dormant, ready, and willing to be reactivated at any time. It holds no grudges, only love and acceptance. The greater the disconnect between our head (thinking brain) and our heart and gut (intuition), the longer it will take for us to renew and rebuild this ever so important relationship with our intuition. Unfortunately, I didn't have this awareness and slowly over the years, I began saying "No" to the voice within and "Yes" to the opinions and influences of others. Their opinions versus my inner knowing had a greater influence in my decisions. Without knowing it, I gave my power away and silenced my innate wisdom and the self who would keep me safe and on the right path.

Initially, when you first step into the place in between, it might feel scary and uncomfortable. Be gentle with yourself as you travel through this space since it is a continuum. Life has a way of having the same lesson show up in different forms to see if we really have learned the lesson, to see how strong and faithful we are to our own voice, and perhaps to give us a chance to practice what we have learned. Rest assured that while you might think you are in the same place, you are not. The experience is not the same despite its commonalities, and you are not the same person as you were yesterday. Experiences have layers, and you are being presented with the next layer. You have gathered insights and awareness along the way and are ready to see the next piece. Notice the ways it is different and the ways you may be showing up differently and offer gratitude for those changes regardless of how big or small they may be. The different spaces you find yourself in and the experiences that come with them, are simply opportunities for you to get to know your true self; for you to learn, heal and to come face to face with beliefs that no longer serve you. Each experience and each moment brings with it the opportunity to develop the muscle of conscious choice and the opportunity to notice what no longer serves you, let it go and embrace what does. This process leads you to live in your light and a life of truth.

If something in this book resonates with you, helps you to gain a different perspective, and gives you permission to simply feel what you are feeling, then it will have served its purpose and my intent.

Introduction

"If you accept the perspective of another person and adopt it as truth, then you must also be prepared to walk in the shoes she or he is wearing. Before you choose those shoes, be sure to notice if you like where they are going and whether or not it feels right for you."
~ Paula Anstett

How much have we adopted as truth? As a parent, I know my goal is to do the very best for my child and what I bring to the parenting table are the experiences I have had and the beliefs I accepted as truths. This book is not about parenting, but the many questions I have asked myself as a parent was the catalyst. *What makes me react as I do? Why do I say yes to some things and no to others? Why do I insist on some things and let go of others? Why do some words and behaviors push my buttons and create a small inferno within while others flow gracefully through me like water passing over smooth rocks as it makes its way down a river? What is the intent when I parent? Do I expose my child to many experiences with the intent of having her see what feels right and what resonates with her? Or is there a different intention? Do I get in the way of her experiences because of a belief that something needs to look or be a certain way? Am I guiding her toward choices that would fulfill a lost dream of mine?*

As parents, not only is any such action unintentional, but past experiences coupled with a culture that inundates us with messages of how we should show up, live, act, and be, cannot help but influence and affect our parenting. Some of us can buy into it for a portion of our lives, maybe even for most of our lives and for some people what they have been exposed to is a wonderful fit for them. But what about the rest of us? When we feel unsettled and unsatisfied regardless of what we have accomplished in the various areas of our life, is it possible our feelings of discontent are the result of us living according to someone else's beliefs and values instead of our own? Contemplation of how I parent and a search to understand why life didn't feel right for me was the genesis of this book, and it led me to find myself on the ledge of the place in between. In *The Wizard of Oz,* Dorothy went on a great exploration down the yellow brick road, and her many experiences became pieces to a puzzle that revealed she had the answers within. The place in between symbolizes the place between where you are now and where you desire to be. For some, the place they desire might be clearly defined down to the smallest details. For others, it can't be clearly defined at all. For most people, however, the place they desire is a feeling. It's how you want to feel within, not what you want to have.

This book is best read a few pages at a time. You might read some perspective that is completely new to you. Some of it may even feel wrong or push a button or two. Begin to see these as wonderful places and become curious. Allow yourself to explore the thoughts and feelings that are surfacing.

Throughout the book, you will see journal exercises. You might be tempted to skip over these pages. Great learning and wisdom await you, so if you are considering skipping these opportunities for insight, ask yourself if you are serious about wanting to live your greatest life. The learning is in the doing. Create time and space for journaling. Allow yourself the time to pause. Allow your pen to write till it is finished writing. You are worthy and deserving of this time and if you truly want some answers, don't skip these pages. Sit with a question. Allow time and space for insights and awareness to come. Let it come without judgment or trying to make sense of it. Notice where it leads you and the feelings that surface and, notice where in your body you feel them.

The Journey Between Places, is a trip down your own yellow brick road. You will explore experiences, thoughts, patterns, and feelings that you have had throughout your lifetime that have led you to where you find yourself today. As you look at them more closely, awareness and insights will come helping you to understand your feelings of discontent. This book is about finding the feeling within that you desire to have.

Get your sparkly red shoes out and let's get started.

Place 1

Is There A Right Time?

"There is always one true inner voice. Trust it."
~ Gloria Steinem

Is there a right time to step into the place in between, or maybe a right status? The very question suggests exploring what "right" means to you. Seldom do the external circumstances ever feel "right," but "where" it feels right is **within**. And while for some, it may feel as though change is forced upon you and out of your control, I have come to learn and respect that everything happens as and when it should, despite it being very hard to embrace this belief at times.

Perhaps the courage to step into the place in between eludes you and then life shows up and makes it happen on your behalf. **Your mindset is the biggest predictor of how life unfolds.** Do you believe that you are a co-creator of your life and therefore contribute to being where you are today? Or do you feel life happens to you? Who are you co-creating your life with? Notice when you are making decisions that are influenced by an outside force versus an inside force, your intuition. Every minute of every day you are making choices. Some of these choices come from your thinking brain. Some occur as a result of following your intuition. Either way, you are at the helm of the choices you make each moment.

Here is an example of how you can co-create with your intuition. Have you ever been en route somewhere and you get a quick message to pop into a bookstore, coffee shop or maybe just take a different route and then something happens that you would have missed had you not listened to the voice within? Sometimes it feels like it doesn't even make sense, but you decide to listen to it anyway. This is an example of co-creating with your intuition. Your intuition is connected to the Universe; when you tap into this rich resource, amazing things happen, and life takes on a beautiful flow. When you believe that you are the one who signs off on every choice, you are fostering a mindset that empowers you. If you believe life happens to you, you are fostering a victim mindset. People with a mindset of empowerment, experience life very differently than people with victim mindsets. People with a mindset of empowerment are excited about each day because they believe they have everything to do with its trajectory.

You might be employed or unemployed, single or married, with or without children. It happens when it happens. If you find this book in your hands, perhaps you can give yourself permission to trust that it is all happening perfectly regardless of where you are in life.

I thought I stepped into the place in between when I left my marriage and while that still feels true, I can see there is a continuum. And even though a specific period of time can punctuate a section on the continuum, life that happens before it has led you to that marked space and time in life. Looking back, I can see how shifts in thoughts, awareness, and choices led me toward what I consider to be the true place in between for me. Entry into the place in between can be marked by a significant event that takes place and creates a major turning point in life. Often, the event that takes place changes the trajectory of your life in some capacity and is a moment in time that is etched in your mind and forever remembered. Sometimes the event occurs through conscious choice. And sometimes, a tipping point is reached, and like a rain cloud that can no longer hold its contents, change cannot be held back. Sometimes it may seem that a seemingly unconnected event brings forth the change. What leads each of us to the place in between is as unique as the individual because I see it being connected to our purpose as well as any healing we need to do in order to fulfill that purpose.

My journey toward the place in between was dotted with daily feelings of being unsettled and unsatisfied in my life, and in particular, in my marriage. What I was missing was intangible because it was a feeling that I desired. By cultural standards, I seemed to have the "perfect" life, but a perfect life has less to do with what you have than what you feel. Deep within I knew something physical wouldn't fill the need I desired, but how do you explain that to people born and raised in a culture where things bring happiness, and a person should be grateful for a beautiful home, a good job, and a husband? I noticed how I started to keep my feelings to myself to avoid judgments and comments from people suggesting nothing was ever good enough for me and that I was never happy despite what I had.

Deep within, I knew there was a missing piece, and I was committed to understanding the unsatisfied longing within. Something didn't "feel" right and despite being very articulate, words that would create understanding of this feeling within, escaped me. Any words that came seemed to fall on deaf ears, and all that could be heard was that I was never happy.

I was unwilling to accept the judgments and criticisms I received as truths (though I have to say that got harder and harder to do with each passing year), and my commitment to understanding what was going on within, grew. Deep within, something didn't feel right, and my thinking brain wanted to make sense of it. There was a need to put words to it. Since then, I have learned that feelings can defy words, and as such, you need to honor your feelings - whether or not your logical brain agrees. I spent years trying to understand what I was feeling on an intellectual level and endlessly searched for a theory that would explain the feelings I felt within. My insatiable desire for an answer and the belief it was external to me was evidenced by the stacks of self-help books that decorated my nightstand and formed tablecloths on the other tables in our house. I was committed to finding the piece of information that would create the life changing "ah-ha" revelation I so desperately sought. I gained tremendous knowledge during this quest which advanced both my intrapersonal and interpersonal awareness and my skills, but the piece of information I desired was yet to be found.

Now I can see that I was looking in the wrong place.

You never know where or when the "ah-ha" moment will appear, but if you don't give up on the quest for it and are open to receiving it - your "ah-ha" moment will eventually appear, and as always, it will appear at the right time and place in life. I realize the many experiences and teachings I had were in preparation for the next ones I would have. I couldn't go to high school without completing grade school. This understanding helps me to see that all experiences have a purpose and significance in our life. Under the rubble and pain lies a gift, a nugget.

One day, I arrived at a place and time when I was ready to hear the message offered to me. It came from a respected marriage and family therapist who was days away from retiring and who clearly knew how to cut to the chase. After a very short time together, she blurted out with confidence and certainty that I had done all my work and half of his. I needed to get on with my life, and it was up to him whether or not he wanted to be in this marriage. I couldn't make him show up.

Wow. As someone who gives a lot of thought to things, sometimes to a detriment, I found much to ponder in the therapist's career closing statement. I could make it about him, but it wasn't about him. It was about me. The words, "I needed to get on with my life" vibrated through me like a bell continues to ring long after it has been struck. My daily "to-do's" centered around fixing our marriage. *What would my days look like If I wasn't spending my time and energy in search of a solution? What would I read in the morning, or while I was eating lunch, and before turning the lights off at the end of the day? What would I talk about with my friends?*

This led to questions like, *What do I want to do with my life? How do I want to make my way in my life? What is my belief about being a wife and a mother? How are those beliefs getting in the way and contributing to the space*

I find myself in? Let's just say the floodgates opened and without any realization at the time, these meanderings and subsequent action steps led me into what would become a major life changing event and turning point in my life. If you have ever played the game Monopoly, it was like landing on the tile that said, "Go directly to jail. Do not pass go and do not collect $200." I didn't go directly to jail, but I did find myself immediately on the ledge of the place in between. It was frightening just like it would be frightening to think you were headed to jail, however, what I would learn in the months to follow was that it came with the next card you hope to draw when you roll the dice, and that is the "Get out of jail" card. The significant moment in your life, the moment when you find yourself on the ledge of the place in between, becomes forever etched in your mind and sends you willingly or unwillingly into the place in between.

I believe the pivotal statement, "You need to get on with your life" applies in various relationships, not just marriages. Within it lies the question: Are you placing your focus where it needs to be, or does your current focus serve as a distraction and keep you from looking at core beliefs that are affecting your life and the relationships you are in - be it with a partner, friend, family member, co-worker, child or a boss? The latter requires looking within and looking at why you are okay being in any relationship where you are not thriving. Does the relationship foster love for yourself or reinforce being unlovable? How do these feelings create further immobility and fear? Can you see the spiral you found your way onto without your conscious awareness?

When the pain gets too great, you might hear yourself say, "Enough." In some cases, life shows up and says it for you. Either way, the place in between is before you.

With this new awareness, my perspective changed and I knew I had to look deep within and create the life I desired separate from my marriage and family life, trusting that in doing so it would be for the greater good of everyone involved.

My focus switched from fixing our marriage to learning about myself. I had no control over how another person was going to show up, all I could control was how I was going to show up. To say there was the absence of fear at this time would be a lie, but alongside the fear, I noticed a skip in my step and renewed energy. Instead of showing up each day and digging in the same hopeless hole, I found new untended ground. Fertile ground that was waiting to be noticed, explored, and cultivated. It was awaiting new seeds and the watering of those seeds. I felt alive as I began to explore me and what I wanted to do and how I could meet my needs. Again, there wasn't the absence of fear especially when the gremlins showed up and whispered (okay, shouted) words of doubt in my ear. *Who am I to have the life I desire? Do I have a purpose that is of value? Will it allow me to make my way in this world?* Though I was clear on what I didn't want and even what I wanted, I wasn't so clear on the belief that I could make it happen or that I was worthy of it.

I allowed the various feelings to surface and decided to work on welcoming them with compassion and acceptance versus judgment and dismissal. These were my feelings after all, and they held the answers. The many books I read offered perspectives, strategies, and techniques but my feelings held the answers. Learning about myself and exploring my feelings is what the place in between offers; it provides an understanding of who you are, what you want, how you want to show up in life, and the beliefs that created your current life. I learned about the beliefs that were tightly woven into my cells that no longer served me and would need to be released and replaced with new beliefs if I was going to be successful in having the life I desired. Beliefs were at the center of why I was okay with being in places and relationships that didn't serve me. Beliefs were why I dismissed my feelings and acquiesced to the wishes of others. I had my work cut out for me!

My new perspective coupled with reading anything that would help me develop a healthier belief system and learn how to love and honor myself slowly changed my terrain. Just like a farmer reworking the soil in the field and preparing it for planting season, I was doing the same with my belief system. I knew this was the starting point. I didn't know where it would lead, but I was feeling better than I had in years and trusted this wonderful feeling to indicate that I was on the right path and it would take me where I needed to go.

In time, the soil within contained the nutrients needed to say no to what didn't feel right and yes to what did. I was no longer willing to turn a blind eye or have a deaf ear. It does not take years to cultivate new soil. The time it takes, correlates to the strength of your decision to own your life, to trust it will be okay, and to commit to replacing faulty beliefs with new loved-filled beliefs.

I distinctly remember reaching the point where I could no longer live as I was living despite the loss that was inevitable, despite the grief that occupied every cell in my body, despite the fear of the unknown, despite the worry of disappointing others and despite the deep concern I felt about how my decision would affect others, my daughter in particular. As incredulous as all of these feelings and thoughts were, there was a feeling deep within that I was doing the right thing by leaving my marriage. My spirit was dying and leaving was my life preserver.

The place in between is a place people travel through for different reasons. What the space has in common for all is that it is a journey to the self. It involves learning about yourself, building a relationship with yourself, validating and accepting who you are, and befriending and learning to love yourself. It has been some of the hardest work I have done and also the most rewarding and life changing. It has brought understanding, compassion, forgiveness, peace, and joy to my heart and to my day. There are moments filled with lots of fear, but I have learned that courage resides in trust and belief. Daily affirmations offered support and when coupled with one small step, if that was all that was possible, led me from darkness and despair to light and new life. To this day, my mantra continues to be: *Do one thing (regardless of how seemingly small it is) every day to move yourself forward.*

Open Your Journal

- Describe one or more things in your lie that doesn't feel right to you.

- What are some things you hear yourself justifying? It could be something you do or something someone else does that deep within you don't like, but you find words and thoughts to justify them.

- Notice when you check out. This is when you do something to escape your current moment or attempt to feel better such as eating, drinking, drugs, TV, talking with friends, even excessive exercise or work often are attempts for us to make sense of something that doesn't feel right, numb it or escape it all together.

Place 2

Creating Separateness

"What someone says, tells me where they are at.
How I respond, tells me where I am at."
~ Paula Anstett

As I traveled through the place in between, it felt incredibly right to remain single, especially after my separation. I was very intentional about not entering a relationship. I felt the need to understand myself, heal wounds, and explore the beliefs charting the course of my life without interference. I guess I am not the multitasker I claim to be! In truth, more recently I am seeing the benefit and the ease of doing one thing at a time though this isn't always realistic or possible. Traveling through the place in between is possible when you are in relationship. It requires strong communication and being intentional to create the separateness you need. Some partners honor this. Others find it unnerving. For those whose wedding vows read, "And two should become one," there may be some difficulty, even guilt, as you begin creating the time and space you need within your relationship. Some people receive wonderful support from their partners, and the relationship creates a safe place to explore your inner world. Can you see there is no right answer, only a right answer for you? You will know which one you have by how you feel. Let your intuition guide you. Continue to affirm being worthy of that which you desire.

When you are on your own, there is no one to blame and no one to project your feelings onto. If only he did this, then I could do that. For years, I focused on fixing a relationship when instead, I should have been exploring and fixing the relationship I had with myself. I did have a pile of self-help books and read them with the goal of figuring out what I was doing wrong, what we were doing wrong and what we needed to change. What I negated to explore was *Why was I okay being in a less than relationship? Why did I stop listening to my intuition? Why was I being pulled into society's belief of how things should look, despite it feeling so wrong to me? Why did I not feel deserving of being loved in a way that felt good and right for me?* What diversion do you have?

I needed to pull myself out of all of this and explore how I got to where I was. *What were the beliefs I was living my life by that not only no longer served me, but never did so in the first place? When did I stop loving myself and allow myself to be treated in a disrespectful way? When did I stop acknowledging, accepting and embracing who I was?* I was a bit surprised to unveil how far back those feelings began. It helped explain my rebellion as a teen and even as a young child. It helped explain the anger that was so close to the surface for as long as I can remember. Many knew it didn't take much to set me off. Finally, I understood the anger. Yes, I was filled with anger, and the anger served as protection; it protected whatever little sense of self I had left. If I could allow myself to be who I was, without needing to explain, justify or defend, there would be no need for the protection and in turn, no need for the anger. In the absence of being able to honor who I was, the best I could do was rebel against who I didn't want to be. While in the place in between, I learned there is value in embracing who I am and leaving behind what I am not, and this includes the life I do not want. I needed love, kindness, and acceptance, instead of criticism and judgment. I was no longer willing to deny my feelings or that which I desired. I learned my outside world was simply a reflection. The change needed to start with me. I needed to stop the criticism and judgment. I needed to give more kindness and acceptance to myself. First and foremost, I needed to say yes to the child within with love and confidence. What others did in response, was not mine to own. I was responsible for myself.

How do you protect yourself? Depression, excessive focus on career, obsession with exercise, drugs, alcohol, anger, withdrawal and eating disorders are some of the many means used to protect yourself. My current understanding of the law of attraction and the power of our thoughts and how they create our life has helped me understand why my life unfolded as it did. Using anger and rebellion as my coping mechanism brought forth more for me to rebel against, more things for me to criticize and more anger within instead of more love.

For change to take place, it is essential to become aware of how your thoughts and feelings are creating your life. Secondly, you have to decide: decide you are ready to see things differently, to show up differently, to break current habits that don't bring the results you desire, to let go of beliefs that no longer serve you and replace them with beliefs that do, and to take appropriate action to "turn the Titanic," as I often refer to it. Change takes time. It starts with a decision and is followed by action. Over time, significant change can and will take place if you continue taking steps, regardless of how big or small, toward the life you desire. Never underestimate the ripple effect of a seemingly small step in the right direction. Doing one small thing every day over the course of a year adds up to 365 action steps. If I asked you if doing 365 things to move yourself forward would make a difference, I'm sure you would say yes. **Who has time or energy to do 365 things all at once? Do one today. Tomorrow, do another one. It adds up. Trust me.**

By remaining single, I found it easier to seize the opportunity to explore the various feelings that came: anger, fear, grief, and joy. There was a mosaic of feelings. At one point, I realized that joy and grief hold hands. When you allow yourself to feel grief, anger, and fear, these feelings get released, and joy awaits you. When we don't allow ourselves to feel and release these feelings, joy continues to sit in the wings, never getting its rightful turn.

There was another reason I saw benefit in remaining single as I traveled through the place in between and it too was linked to my belief in the law of attraction. If I believed that my thoughts and feelings were linked to what I attracted into my life, then given my current thoughts and feelings, it was likely that I would attract a person who was angry and filled with grief, or on the flip side, wanting to rescue me and make it all better. I didn't see either of these scenarios creating the life I desired to have. I held the belief that to have the life I desired, I first needed to look within. When a friend asked if I would ever date again, this was my response, "For sure I will. I want to have something positive to talk about when he asks how my day is going. I also want everything in the baggage I am carrying to be washed, air dried and bringing value to my next relationship." Currently, that isn't the case. His question came while I was going through a very challenging divorce, and daily there were dealings that were disturbing and created significant upset and anger.

Some might say, "Wouldn't it have been nice to have support during such a time?" and for some, that might be the case which is why I say there is no right or wrong way to proceed. Support is one thing, as having someone hold the space for you could be comforting. However, being under the illusion that someone else can make every awful feeling in your present go away and make you happy is another. For me, since I was already hurting and confused, I didn't want to take any chance that I wouldn't know the difference. I wanted to be "clearer" entering the next relationship. I wanted to feel love and compassion, not anger and fear. I wanted to be on steady ground in every area of my life. I wanted to love myself and my life. I wanted to feel complete and whole, and I believed when the timing was right it would happen quite organically. I continued walking my path.

That was me.

For others, the experience can be different. Maybe a person comes into your life and is a positive influence as you walk through the place in between. Maybe you choose to walk the path with a current or new partner, and through the process become stronger as individuals, and as a couple. For some, a current or new relationship may have served its purpose and needs to end. There is no right or wrong. There is value in being aware of what the person represents and how the relationship serves you. It is common to attract what you know so even though the person and relationship may seem very different, it might be the same or have many commonalities. Sometimes you intentionally attract the exact opposite, determined to never again have what you had, only to find a complete pendulum shift can bring other challenges. If the law of attraction holds true, you will likely attract what aligns with your current way of thinking and feeling. Awareness is key.

Here is another thought to ponder: Is the desire to date and have a partner linked to the new space you are in feeling foreign and uncomfortable? Despite not wanting to have what you had, there is comfort in having what you know. It compares to the comfort you feel slipping into an old pair of shoes versus a brand-new pair. Comfort sometimes wins out. Perhaps you are afraid to "feel" the feelings that are surfacing, so a diversion (being in relationship with someone else versus yourself) is easier. It's easier to look at what he / she needs to do or change than what you need to do or change. What is showing up for you when you are with this person? What are they offering you? Is this something you need to offer to yourself? Why does it keep you from looking at within? How do you describe him or her? So often I have heard people say how the person makes them feel. What happens when someone no longer makes you feel this way? What's left? Also, can you show up completely transparent in the relationship or do you fear losing the person and therefore losing the feeling you are receiving?

Put another way, what do you feel is missing in your life? How do you want to feel? What kind of feeling do you find yourself seeking within the relationship? Is it really missing, or is it an unclaimed part of yourself?

If you are in the place in between and aspire to go somewhere different than from where you came, is it possible to attract the person you desire to attract if you are not yet that person? Can you receive what you desire if you are not yet in the space of feeling worthy and able to receive? Maybe or maybe not. These are simply thoughts to consider and keep in your awareness. Maybe a person comes into your life and offers the compassion, strength, and support you need until you build your own. Maybe they give you permission to welcome the person you desire to be with gentleness, not judgment, recognizing the journey to the self takes time, expression of feelings, and healing. Maybe you prefer to be on your own. There isn't a right or wrong way. What's important is to have awareness. Notice your actions. Listen to your words. They hold the clues to the motivation behind your current actions. Above all, be mindful to avoid anyone who doesn't want you to step into your worthiness.

Shortly after separating, these words by Shakti Gawain came to me, *"The qualities that women have looked for in men - strength, power, responsibility, caring, excitement, romance-must be developed inside of ourselves. A simple formula is this: just treat yourself exactly the way you would want to be treated by a man."*

A woman's power lies deep within. Her intuition is her power source, and when honored and trusted, it provides the strength she needs. From this place, she can be compassionate, caring and live an unbridled life filled with excitement, passion, and romance.

I encourage you to embrace the most important relationship of all: the one you have with yourself. Whether you do this while on your own or while in a relationship, it doesn't matter. What matters is that you discover who you are and learn to love yourself. If you need some clues on how to get started, think about what you do and say when you are dating and getting to know someone. Do you dress differently, eat differently, or act differently? Do you buy yourself something new to wear? Is it time to start dressing up for you? Treat yourself the way you want to be treated. What are you looking for in a partner? Become that person. Allow yourself to be and have that which you desire.

If a beautiful, loving, respectful, kind, open, and honest relationship is what you desire, it has to start with having that kind of relationship with yourself.

Open Your Journal

- If you are in a relationship or seeking a relationship, what do you hear yourself saying you want from the relationship?

- Describe his / her qualities and characteristics.

- What values are important to you?

- Complete the following sentences:
  a. I like him / her because…
  b. I wish he / she would…
  c. If only he / she did… then I would…

- Looking at your above answers, do you possess the things you want? What do you need to do to develop the qualities and characteristics you are seeking to find in a partner?

- Make a list of the things you would do if you just met someone new and began dating them such as buying a new outfit, doing your nails, etc. Make another list of things that would make you feel appreciated and special if they did them. Close your eyes and visualize the perfect date if that helps to get your imagination going. Post these lists somewhere visible to you (maybe on your bathroom mirror! Whiteboard markers work great!) and commit to dating yourself and giving yourself what you want someone else to give you.

Place 3

Chaos – Finding Hope Within It

"Sometimes, in order to be happy in the present moment, you have to give up the hope for a better past."
~ Robert Holden

What can you expect to experience when you step into the place in between? For each person, the experience will be unique. For all people, there will be a level of chaos, an inevitable state that occurs when you change what is currently familiar and the norm, even if the place you occupy allows you to thrive or is damaging to your spirit. Familiar and the norm are not synonymous with thriving.

For some, it can start out being incredibly chaotic. There are many factors that contribute to the degree of chaos you experience which include whether the change comes upon quickly or if there is adequate transition time. How prepared are you? How prepared are the people in your life who will also be affected by the change? Do you have positive and encouraging people in your life or people who are critical and judgmental? How do you handle change? Do you have effective coping strategies? The degree to which the change will affect other areas of your life, the onset of change and whether you or someone else initiated the change are additional factors. Did it happen gradually or suddenly? Were you prepared or blindsided? Even when a plan is in place, and you feel ready and prepared, reality is always different, and feelings and circumstances are often greater than what you perceived and prepared yourself for.

For some, stepping into the place in between can mean significant change and / or loss in one or more areas of your life: relationship, financial, where you live, your health, or your work. Maslow's hierarchy of needs[1] outlines that we need to have our basic needs met before we can work on other higher levels of being.

Where do you find yourself right now? It is important to recognize and honor the needs of this space. If you have lost basic needs such as food, shelter, safety and security, the level of chaos you experience is likely elevated as are feelings of anxiety and fear. It is important to give yourself permission to be where you are today and to focus on regaining the safety and security that comes with having these basic needs in place. It doesn't matter where you were before or what you had before, there is no value in judgment and criticism. There is value in accepting, trusting, and being where you are today.

Many people live in cultures that fail to honor this process or grant the time needed to feel, heal, reestablish and rebuild. Daily life continues. Children need to be cared for, bills have to be paid, and work obligations need to be met. Maybe the change you experienced requires you to find new work or a means to survive. It is easy to see how chaos is imminent, and it is normal to feel a bit overwhelmed and have some level of anxiety. Such feelings come when you may be feeling a loss of control or uncertainty about your future. Being kind to yourself, asking for what you need, and allowing others to help is especially important during such times. Reaching out, putting some things on the back burner while you re-establish and rebuild is not only okay, but fundamental. **Give yourself the permission to do what you need to do and feel what you need to feel. Your perception and mindset have a significant effect on your ability to proceed. Trust that you have what it takes to move through this space. Trust that all is going to work out.**

---

1 McLeod, S. A. (2016). Maslow's Hierarchy of Needs. Retrieved from www.simplypsychology.org/maslow.html

Trust you will get to higher ground. Use affirmations multiple times a day and positive self-talk to nourish your belief in yourself.

Your mindset, the beliefs you possess, and your threshold of acceptance affect how you move forward. These elements may not take away the sense of loss or fear you feel, but they can create the understanding, strength, courage, and conviction you need to get up each day and continue on. There is no need or value in judging or criticizing yourself or the space you find yourself in. To do so is damaging and potentially paralyzing. Accepting and embracing where you are does not mean that you are going to be in this space forever, rather it is through acceptance that you will find the courage, strength, and energy needed to start taking the necessary action steps to move yourself forward. It isn't possible to move forward when you are in a state of resistance. If you are unwilling to accept where you are then you are resisting where you are. Resistance is like having your foot on the brake of your car. Acceptance moves your foot from the brake to the gas pedal.

My motto during a tumultuous and debilitating time was to do one thing every day to move myself forward. Holding onto and living true to this one motto allowed me to rise out of the space I was in and into a much better space, not overnight but over time. Many days it did not seem as though doing one thing would ever be enough to make a difference but I stayed committed to the practice. Some days my one thing could be as small as leaving a single voicemail, but in my world, it counted. Many days it was all I could muster, so I counted it and celebrated it. It continues to be a ritual I practice today.

Metaphors and analogies create pictures in my mind and seem to bring understanding and vision. Here is one that worked for me. Picture a home you desire to have. Fill in as many details as you can. Now, make the decision to build it. When you declare you are going to build it, do you hear the immediate reasons why it is not possible to do so? I call this monkey chatter, and it might be telling you that you don't have the time, money or knowledge to build it. Maybe you lack all three at this time. While you might agree, you decide you are willing to learn, and you will search for the resources you need. You begin to share your goal with some people. Some people laugh at you, seeing your goal is audacious. Some people offer to help in any way they can. And some people feel sorry for you thinking you will never have what you desire.

In fact, you too will admit that sometimes you wonder if you can do it, especially on the days when life throws some new challenges your way, but you stay true to your commitment and your desire. You commit to doing one thing a day. At the beginning, you focus on gathering the information you need. Eventually, the hole for the house is dug, the foundation poured, and you finally get to the bricklaying phase. You commit to laying ten bricks a day. That's all the time you have. Despite the comments you hear, both from your inner and outer worlds, you continue on. Over time and distance, the home you desired and held in your vision is created, and you see what is possible when you commit to doing what you can each day. You recall days when you only laid one brick and days when you laid twenty. You honored the energy you had on those days, and despite wavering energy, your belief, hope, and positive mindset remained intact. You celebrated every action, big or small and at the end of every day expressed gratitude for what you were capable of doing. There were days when people showed up to help, and you graciously accepted. Some days, a phone call filled with encouraging words provided the fuel you needed that day. And sometimes, there were days no one was there to offer support physically or emotionally, and you dug deep within and found the courage and energy you needed to do one thing.

Building a home can create a visual of what rebuilding your life after change looks like. There is knowledge to acquire, steps to take, actions to implement. Maybe your life resembles a renovation, and there is much to clean out before new building can take place. Either way, life continues on and sometimes throws us a few more curveballs along the way. If you watch any of the home shows currently on television, the contractors always run into a glitch. The project never goes smoothly from beginning to end. Do they throw in the towel or find a solution? They look for options. Sometimes it requires looking at something differently than how they initially envisioned it.

Sometimes it requires additional work and money. They have to be willing to make changes so they can continue on. Similarly, you too may experience a few curveballs along the way. Do they knock you off your path, divert your attention, or cause you to question your quest? Or do they bring forth new thoughts and feelings that you use moving forward? In my experience, they always brought forth learning opportunities. See more about this in Place 4, titled, *It's Great Information*.

Open Your Journal

- What is one thing you can do today to move yourself forward?

- What is one piece of information you need to help you move forward?

- Create a gratitude journal. Every day, write 3 things for which you are grateful. Expressing gratitude for even the smallest of things will create a positive feeling within and bring about more abundance in your life.

- Write 3 successes you had today. Many successes go unnoticed and unrecognized. It doesn't matter how big or small the action is. The truth is, they are all big.

It has been said that as long as you have a smidgen of hope, you will continue on. In the dictionary, hope is defined as, *"The feeling that what is wanted can be had, or that events will turn out for the best."* Experts in the field of mental health and treatment of addiction know that hope is a major cornerstone for recovery. In the absence of hope, there is no motivation to get better or to keep going. Without motivation, there is no action. Without action, there is no improvement. [2]

---

2 Edgewood Health Network (n.d.) The Importance Of Hope In Addiction Recovery. Retrieved from http://edgewood-healthnetwork.com/blog/the-importance-of-hope-in-addiction-recovery

During this time, it is important to nourish yourself with books, audios and people who help instill a feeling of hope. Jim Rohn says, *"You are the average of the five people you spend the most time with."* With whom do you spend the most time? Remember, authors can make up these five people! Choose wisely with whom you spend your time, your life depends on it. If there are a lot of negative people in your life or people who are not supportive of your desires, choose to minimize your time with them. If at this time, you don't have positive, encouraging and supportive people you can turn to, there is a vast array of inspirational authors and speakers that you can choose to plug into until such time that you begin to attract wonderful, loving and supportive people. The world is filled with such people you just have to love yourself enough to feel worthy of them and open yourself up to allowing and receiving such people into your life! What a difference it has made in my life! **You feed your physical body food every day. What are you feeding your mind? Your mind needs daily nourishment too.** Let's look at how perception and mindset have a major influence on how our lives play out.

For almost three decades, I have read and been wonderfully influenced by Louise Hay's work. I credit her teachings and my willingness to practice them for the place I find myself today. Some might call me a slow learner but learning is a process, and there are many layers to penetrate. Each time I reread one of her books, her messages have a new meaning. You can't build the second floor of your house without first laying the foundation and building the first floor. If you are planning to build a high rise you can reread the book with each new floor you build and receive new information.

Do you believe you have created the life you have right now because of how you think? How do you answer that question and what feelings surface? Do you feel defensive and at fault for where you are today or do you feel confident because you see yourself as the master creator of your life? This one question can have two completely different answers and create two completely different outcomes for your life. The first perspective takes your power away, the other empowers you. Instead of going through life blaming and being victimized, you can see there is always a choice. Just this one perspective shift will change your life immeasurably. Moreover, when you own your thoughts and feelings, you, not someone else, are at the helm of your life. Hopelessness occurs when you feel things won't or can't change. When you take responsibility for your thoughts and feelings, you will always feel hopeful. You are the master creator of your life! I realize, and know all too well, that at times of change and chaos it is difficult to know where to start, but know that you can make a decision to start. As philosopher Lao-Tzu says, *"The journey of a thousand miles begins with a single step."*

My first step was to mind my mind. I began to notice my thoughts. I noticed which thoughts served me, and which did not. I decided to think positively and to take the high road. Actions I took would be for my betterment and to move me forward versus to cause pain or detriment to others. My focus was on creating the life I wanted. How many times do we spend valuable time rehashing old stuff, trying to be right or hurt someone who hurt us? What a waste of valuable energy! Perhaps this is the route you take when you don't know where you want to go and maybe it serves to keep you from looking at what you want and deciding to create it. Maybe it feels like the easier path. Wherever you find yourself, start with changing your thoughts. This is the most important and powerful step you will ever take, and it is the cornerstone for moving through the chaos.

Changing how you think costs no money yet yields so much - all it requires is a willingness and a decision to think differently. Immediately you will begin charting a new course! Make it a daily practice to mind your thoughts and to learn to love yourself and you are on your way to a wonderful place! Commit to the process. Change may take time, but it is possible. I want to share two affirmations from Louise Hay's *You Can Heal Your Life* that will help get you started:

"Every thought we think is creating our future."

"When we really love ourselves, everything in our life works."

Back to Maslow's hierarchy of needs. Be cognizant that we cannot achieve all levels at once or in reverse order. I live in Canada, and for the most part, it seems our culture has adopted a right now, multitasking way of living. When setting out to achieve any goal, it is important to see the value of determining priority and maintaining focus. Let's say that you have decided (everything starts with a decision) to be mindful of your thoughts and adopt the practice of positive thinking. The next step might be to look at what you need to do to get through your day. If your world has been turned upside down, then looking at how you will get through your day might very well be enough. Remember, it's one step at a time and one day at a time.

I'm going to break it down even further because there was a time when looking at the entire day was too much for me. Do you feel that way? I remember feeling so overwhelmed, but what helped me cope was breaking my day into four-hour chunks.

I started looking at my day and asking myself, *What do I have to do to get through the next four hours?* There is a saying that, *"The way to eat an elephant is one bite at a time."* How much does one bite contain for you right now? What is manageable for you? A good way to determine the size of your bite is to see if it allows you to take action or does it immobilize you? If it immobilizes you, it's too big. If it creates anxiety, it's too big. Break it down until you arrive at a place that allows you to cope and take action. Avoid judging the size of the bite. Size is not important. Being able to take action is. This strategy proved to be incredibly valuable, and when done without judgment, you move forward. What do I mean when I say, "without judgment?" I mean without any negative self-talk. Maybe at one time in your life, you could do much more. It doesn't matter. Today is today, and with it comes a different situation and experience. Maybe your thoughts are self-defeating in another way. **Be where you are without judgment. Do what you can and celebrate any and every act you do to move yourself forward.**

Despite being in a much better place than when I first started writing this book, there are days and hours during the day, when I have too much to do. I have evolved this practice. I have learned to take a deep breath and remind myself that if I remain calm and focused, everything goes better. I ask myself, *What needs to get done in the next 15 minutes?* Then I put my blinders on. I'm telling you, it works! Decide what works for you. There are days when you might need to look at your day 15 minutes at a time, in two-hour chunks or maybe you divide the day into morning, afternoon and evening. Do what feels right and works for you. Different days might require different kinds of time chunking. It's okay. Remember, no judgment or criticism, right? This entire book is about giving yourself permission to honor where you are and offers tools and insights on how to move forward, one step at a time. It is better to do one small thing that only requires five minutes of your time and leaves you either in the same place or a better place emotionally than when you first started, rather than attempting to do more than you can handle only to feel defeated, frustrated, and more depleted. Honor where you are at and applaud all efforts, even those that seem insignificant because, in truth, they are the most significant.

Have you ever heard yourself compare what you are able to do today with what you did years ago? Was it a valuable exercise? Another saying I have is, *"If you are going to compare something in your life, you have to compare all the components around it too."* You are never in the same place with all variables being the exact same so to compare where you are today with any other time in your life is pointless and usually damaging. This also holds true if you are considering comparing yourself to someone else. Unless you can compare every variable, don't bother, and the reality is, you can't compare every variable so don't bother trying. Don't believe me? Start by comparing your genetic makeup. Do you need eight hours of sleep while someone else thrives on five hours each night? Enough said. Don't compare.

Decide to stop all comparison and all criticism. Neither is conducive to forward movement and fostering self-love. Instead, recognize there is tremendous value in taking any step regardless of how big or small the step is and being grateful for your ability to do so. Over time these individual steps will add up and lead you to be in a better place both physically, mentally and emotionally.

"Each step you take reveals a new horizon. You have taken that first
step today. Now I encourage you to take another."
~ Dan Poynter

In summary, what does your place of chaos look and feel like? Are
you willing to commit to doing one thing each day, however big or
small, to move yourself through it? Sometimes that one thing may
only take a minute or two and if that is all the time you have or all the
energy you have, celebrate and be grateful for your accomplishment.
Gratitude brings more to be grateful for and being kind to yourself
is key to the healing process. If a young child was struggling, would
you show kindness, gentleness and offer encouragement? Would you
applaud and celebrate any effort, big or small that she made? Or,
would you criticize and berate her for not doing enough? Can you
see the small child within yourself? What does she need to hear? Be
gentle and kind with yourself. Give yourself permission to be where
you are today. Acknowledge every step, every effort, regardless of
perceived size for they are all big and significant.

Open Your Journal

In the last chapter, you looked at one thing you could do to move
yourself forward, and you are going to continue that process in this
chapter (and hopefully forever!) with the focus being on what you
are thinking and with whom you are spending your time.

• Begin noticing your thoughts. This practice alone will change
  your life because you will begin to see what is swimming around
  in your head and affecting your day and ultimately your life.
  Awareness is the first step toward change so when you hear any

criticism or self-defeating talk, interrupt it and replace it with encouraging, supportive words.

- Affirmations are food for your brain. Start your day saying them, carry them with you and read them throughout your day (write them on the back of a business card or on a small piece of paper) and end your day saying them. Your brain is a like a muscle that you are retraining. Once a day isn't enough. Write five affirmations with words that will serve you. You can rewrite as required.

- Create one or more affirmations to support where you are at this time. Here are some examples.

  "I speak only kind and loving words to myself and about myself."

  "Each day I do one thing, big or small, to move myself forward."

  "I am doing the best I can."

- Three of Louise Hay's affirmation that I continue to use are:

  "I love and approve of myself."

  "I am safe."

  "Life loves me."

  Repeat the affirmations - "I am safe," and "Life loves me," throughout your day. Say them as soon as you wake up and before you go to sleep. Whenever you feel anxious, repeat them until the anxiety subsides. It works!

- Make a list of the people with whom you spend the most time. Put a star beside the people who are supportive and helpful to you and who feed your spirit. Put an X beside those who do not. Commit to reducing the time spent with the people who have an X beside their name. Even if you live with these people, it is possible to reduce the amount of time you spend with them.

- Become a reader. What are you currently reading? I have included a great selection of books at the back of this book. Pick the one that catches your attention. Let your intuition make the selection.

Place 4

It's Great Information

"Because the greatest part of a road trip isn't arriving at your destination. It's all the wild stuff that happens along the way."
~ Emma Chase

People often hear me say, "That's great information" and often when I say it, it is linked to information some think is not so great. I receive both curious and cautious looks when I say it with such excitement. I feel that whatever comes to you in your day is simply information and I have come to view it as "great information" because there is always a message and a gift that travels on the wings of the experience.

Have you ever been witness to a conversation and listened to or seen two people have completely different reactions to a comment that was made? Different reactions, also known as different perspectives, occur because people have different life experiences and from those experiences develop different knowledge and beliefs. Their knowledge and beliefs create the lens from which they process information and how they view life. Maybe you have heard the expression, *"She sees things through rose colored glasses."* What color are the glasses you look through? And what has colored them? Since no two people have had the exact same experiences in life, it makes sense that everyone looks at things a little differently. This makes for an interesting and diverse world, and when you are open, receptive, and willing to listen without judgment or defensiveness, conversation can flow more easily, even when someone thinks and feels something differently than you do.

When a conversation doesn't flow smoothly but rather pushes a button, are you able to step out of it and see what is going on? This can be very difficult to do when it is in full swing. There's an expression, *"That hit a nerve."* What nerve did the comment hit? What interpretation did you make that others may not have made?

Before understanding that a past experience is what triggers the way I react, interact, and interpret a situation or conversation, I became defensive, even combative, as a means of making my story right or relieving the pain that was triggered. While these responses may have provided some temporary relief, I missed the opportunity to see the great information that was underneath the feelings. In truth, there wasn't even temporary relief if I walked away feeling anything but peace within. When you react to a comment versus explore the feeling you are experiencing, you miss seeing the gift it holds and the opportunity to explore the belief and the hurt you are holding onto.

Open Your Journal

- Think back to a situation, event or conversation that pushed your buttons. What did the person say?

- What did you hear? In other words, what was your interpretation of what was said?

- What feelings did you experience?

- Where does the thought take you? Can you link it to something that happened at another time in your past? If your thoughts and feelings are attached to a previous experience can you see how they are perspective (something based on an experience) versus a fact?

When buttons get pushed, you might receive a wide range of messages. On one end, you might learn there is another belief that needs to be explored and resolved. You may need to feel a past hurt so you can let it go. Maybe it sheds light on your desire to create a new belief that serves you better. On the other end, a pushed button may signify your readiness to say, "Enough." If you reached the point of enough, what have you had enough of?

Your feelings are one of the ways your body communicates with you. On any given day, you can feel uneasy, excited, motivated, unmotivated, tingly, ill, low energy, high energy, sad or angry to name just a few. The list could go on. I believe feelings contain great information. It's easy to accept the feelings that make you feel good, but what about the ones that stir emotion? What would your day and life look like if you chose to see your thoughts and feelings as good information, an opportunity to get to know and understand yourself, your beliefs and the thoughts you have linked to your feelings?

When you step into your day with this mindset, the day unfolds in a completely different way. You are empowered, not victimized. You become a student of life, and the messages life brings to you. The information you receive might show you what you need to learn, what you need to heal or what you need to allow or not allow into your life. For instance, you find yourself in a situation at work where you don't know the answer to something that others feel you should be well versed in. What is your response? What feelings arise inside? Your response holds messages, and it also creates your life moving forward. Do you criticize the person who asked you the question? Do you criticize yourself for not knowing the answer? Maybe you try to come up with something on the spot. Or, do you say with confidence, "Great question. I don't know, but I will find out." If you felt embarrassed, can you acknowledge that feeling versus criticizing yourself? Can you connect your present feeling of embarrassment with a time in your past when you were embarrassed? How many unresolved experiences are buried within and when you least expect it, they are brought back into the light?

Wayne Dyer says, *"When we change the way we look at things, the things we look at change."* How you respond to an experience holds great information and often shines light on what you need to learn next, and sometimes what you need to resolve or heal. In the above example, do you set out to get the answer with interest or begrudgingly? Maybe you need to look at where you felt embarrassed in the past and the circumstances around that experience. If you were humiliated, it can be helpful and healing to acknowledge the feeling and the experience so you can let it go. If you cannot move forward in your present day, something needs to be resolved. You have a choice in how you view the incident and how you respond, as not only does how you respond affect your immediate day, it also affects your life. I have seen this play out in my own life.

I was doing a presentation, and someone asked me about a line of our products that I didn't know as well as I thought I did. In that moment, I remember feeling inadequate and unprofessional. I did my best to offer what knowledge I had, but deep within I knew the truth and the truth was that I had no clue. As I walked toward my car, I had a choice in what I would say to myself and how I would feel. I said with conviction and kindness, "That will never happen to me again." This was a kind and proactive response. What if my response was critical and self-defeating? If I chose to be critical, it held great information. The first step would be to stop the criticism and open up to the pain. Where did I feel this way before? What did I stuff down and not resolve or forgive at that time? Who spoke those words to me in the past?

I was grateful that I spoke kind words to myself and committed to seeking the knowledge I lacked. I saw it as an opportunity to learn, grow, and move my business forward, and that it did. It didn't go unnoticed that in the past, my reaction would have been different and I took the time to acknowledge and celebrate the gains I have made. (Reminder - celebrate all successes!). My progress was linked to the healing and growing I had done to date. I recall thinking, *It's finally starting to show up in my day.* My efforts to feel, heal and release were beginning to bear fruit, and this sure put a skip in my step! The next day I made some calls, and in a short time, I was given a referral. I contacted the person and hired her on an hourly basis to teach me what I needed to learn. *Perfect,* I thought, and I quickly secured an appointment with her. I happily and willingly chose to pay for the knowledge I wanted. I was taking full responsibility for my business and what I needed to learn to have the success I desired. There was no complaining about the cost or why it was mine to pay.

During our time together, I learned a great deal. Something that neither of us expected to learn was how the business I had could benefit her. Within the same month, this woman who I hired, ended up joining my business. Did I see that coming? Never. Did I hire her hoping she would join me in business? No. The course of events happened because of how I responded to a very embarrassing and frustrating moment. I chose to take responsibility and to see the event as a learning opportunity. My positive response not only allowed me to learn something new, but it also brought a new inspiring person into my life who has become both a colleague and a treasured friend.

Think about how my reaction to the experience could have played out differently. I could have chosen to complain about the people who attended the presentation and their lack of interest in our signature products - products I knew well. I could have blamed the company for not insisting that I do the training I was lacking. I could have come up with some excuse to pin on the experience that would allow me to remain a victim versus a hero in my story. I could have started some self-barraging conversation including a plethora of reasons why I would never attain the success I desired. All of these were options, and thankfully they were not on my options list. I saw no value in any response that disempowered me and held no opportunity for me to learn and move me and my business forward. **When you see experiences as great information, offer gratitude for the gift it holds and then take appropriate action, wonderful things come to you.** As I said, the woman I hired is now a treasured friend as well as an inspiring colleague, and I feel blessed to know her. She has been a wonderful influence both on my daughter and to many in my organization. I am grateful to know her and to have her and her family in my life.

Think about how the course of events in your life and your life as you know it, have been created because of how you responded to the events that take place. If after the presentation, I kicked myself to the car and criticized the people for the questions they asked me, my life stood little chance of improving, and chances are I would have continued on a downward spiral. The feelings I had were real and valid so there was value in feeling them so that I could let them go and move on. It was the action steps I took thereafter that propelled my life forward. And interestingly enough, the outcome of those actions brought forth more great information. It drove home the point that how I view the happenings in my day, and the thoughts I attach to them are how I create my life. Regardless if they are initially perceived as positive or negative, good or bad, they always contain great information and what I do with that information is my choice. Remember, you are at the helm of your life. Find the gift in the situation and say goodbye to bad experiences, for in truth, they are all good when you let them bring good to you.

Open Your Journal

- Think back to a frustrating situation. What happened?

- If you criticized yourself, what did you say?

- Where in your past did you hear those criticisms?

- Feel what you were feeling at the time. When you acknowledge a feeling and then feel it, you can release it.

- Can you forgive the person who uttered the words you have been holding onto? Can you forgive yourself for holding onto those words for so long?

- Rewrite the story in a way that serves your moving forward. Perhaps the incident created resilience or independence. Find a positive that you can extract from the experience even if it is very small. If you look hard enough, you will find a gift!

- Visualize the frustrating experience and insert a new way of responding to it. Picture the new response in as much detail as you can and add feeling to it. This might include thanking the past for what you learned. Maybe it's feeling excited about reacting in a proactive way that serves you and helps you create the life you desire!

Take yourself through this process when you hear negative self-talk. Each time you do, you will be healing old wounds and creating the opportunity for new, empowered actions steps.

Do you think the principle of great information could be used in more dire situations, like a health diagnosis or the end of a marriage? I chose to use it when my marriage ended, and it created the opportunity for me to grow as an individual, forgive myself and others, and create an exceptionally joy-filled life. I didn't deny my feelings. It was essential to feel the anger and grief (rain) before I could fully embrace the information and gifts (rainbow and sunshine) they brought. It was a decision to seek and find the great information that lay deep within the experience. At times, I had to dig deep to find it. But if you hold the mindset that all experiences are happening **for** you; not to you, you will find the gift. There is always a gift. **There is always a piece you can own, and the reward of owning your feelings and your contribution is self-empowerment.**

I have been blessed with good health, but when there is a disturbance in my physical or emotional state, I immediately look at it as great information and begin my exploration of the meaning behind what is presenting. I have resolved debilitating back pain, mouth sores, headaches, low energy and digestive issues using this technique. A dear friend who experienced cancer in her lifetime used this same approach to her healing. She too chose to see what was happening in her body as great information. Her journey was significant, and despite a diagnosis of pelvic and bone cancer which left her in debilitating pain and bedridden, she eventually rode a bike again. She was so clear that the cancer brought with it the information she needed to heal. She experienced this once before in her life and found physical healing through her emotional healing. During our conversations, she would say that if she didn't deal with her anger and resentment, it would cost her, her life.

My dear friend, I honor you and your journey. You taught me that there is value in looking at all experiences, even the really tough ones, as offering great information. You also taught me that while the information comes when you open up to receiving it, healing is only possible when you forgive, let go and replace beliefs that no longer serve you with ones that do. I can only imagine the courage it took to walk your path and will forever honor and respect you and your journey. **Your body is constantly sending you messages via feelings and thoughts. It is my belief that if you learn to honor the voices and feelings from within, you can prevent the volume from being turned up, so to speak.** When you ignore the body's messages, the body has a way of turning up the volume. Why not listen to the nudge? Do you really need to hit a wall, or develop an illness in order to open up to the messages?

Place 5

Becoming Aware Of Your Intuition

"Every time you ask for guidance, you receive it."
~ Gary Zukav

Have you ever lost sleep because you are thinking about a conversation you had with someone? Or maybe, you are working through a feeling that has been lingering within. Have you ever considered that this may be another way your body attempts to deliver great information to you? Next time this happens, instead of being frustrated with your insomnia, consider opening up and honoring the messages your inner self is attempting to communicate. Notice if you feel calmer after reading the last sentence. To ignore your feelings, deny they exist or talk yourself out of feeling them is not an act of self-love. Without it being your intention to do so, you are dishonoring and betraying yourself. No one intentionally does this, but when you silence or scold the feelings that are surfacing, that is exactly what you are doing. If your friend shared such feelings with you, how would you respond? Would you respond with a listening ear and compassion? Do you respond differently to your own feelings?

Did you hear words at a young age and accept them as truth?

These so-called truths became beliefs, and they created rules for your life that you believe are inflexible, much like the rules in a board game. However, whose rules are you playing by? The most life changing belief is any belief which suggests that something or someone outside of you has the answers. This belief silences your intuitive voice and causes you to stop listening to it. Your intuition will always keep you on your intended path when you listen to it. When negated, the doors open for you to stray from a path of respect, love, health, and peace onto a path of dishonor and disrespect for self, others, and life.

Let's go back to the example about losing sleep over a conversation you had with someone and let's look at how the thoughts and feelings you are experiencing simply offer great information. What if, instead of being frustrated that you can't sleep, you relax your body and notice the thoughts and feelings you are having without judgment? This allows you to stay open to what they are attempting to communicate to you. Next time you can't sleep, shift how you view the experience and see what comes.

When you open up to seeing the different ways your body communicates to you (feelings, holding back, lying awake) it allows you to criticize less and be more loving and receptive. Now when I find myself awake in the middle of the night, I thank my subconscious for showing up and stay open to receiving the message it is bringing. The answer usually comes rather quickly and shortly thereafter, I find myself falling asleep. Can you see how lying awake might be your body's way of sending you some great information?

As you rebuild your relationship with your intuition and begin honoring it, your current relationships are likely to be affected. You might begin saying no to things you said yes to in the past or yes to things you have said no to. If you are someone who never expressed your needs and desires and are now becoming more vocal, you might experience some resistance from the people in your life. The people you are in relationships with have grown accustomed to you responding in a certain way. As a result, your conversations have become familiar, much like a well-rehearsed dance. Using dancing as an analogy, picture yourself stepping right when for years you stepped left. It might cause the person you are dancing with to go off balance and maybe even step on your toe. He might feel embarrassed and blame you for stepping the wrong way. If it is a slight misstep, the two of you might be able to seamlessly adjust and resume your dance. But what if you don't want to resume the dance as you have come to know it?

You have taught the people in your life how to treat you, so you have to be mindful to also teach them the new way you want to be treated. When you change how you show up, even ever so slightly, it takes time for the people you are interacting with to know how to respond. Some people will welcome the change. Some will resist the change and prefer things to be as they were. Communication is key.

If you feel resistance as you make changes, you might notice a tendency to revert back to old patterns as a means to avoid conflict. Were you raised hearing the phrase, "keep the peace" even if keeping the peace meant dishonoring your needs? Be mindful of that during this time. Are your actions filled with fear or love? Do you love yourself enough to say no to what no longer feels right for you and yes to what does? Do you fear what will happen if you honor yourself? When people attempt to control you, and when they want you to show up in a particular way that serves them but not you, it is because of their own inner fears and lack of self-love. Notice what is going on and learn to see it as great information. There is no need or value in morphing into something you are not in order to be accepted, keep the peace, or make someone else feel less uncomfortable. To do so serves neither you nor the other person. This principle applies to partners, friends, and family. Continue to practice self-love. The more you do so, the more you can encourage your loved ones and support them to do the same.

Open Your Journal

Think of a time when you said no, when in fact you really wanted to say yes or vice versa. Ask yourself why and what you were feeling at the time and maybe even what you are feeling now at the very thought of it. Write whatever comes. Don't worry about sentence structure, grammar or neatness. Just write.

- What information came to you? Whose voice did you hear?

- What beliefs can you identify?

- What fears showed up?

- Close your eyes and visualize how your life would improve if you did what felt right for you. Get very clear on that vision and engage all of your senses. See it. Feel it. Hear it. Smell it. Touch it.

- Know that you are worthy and deserving of the life you desire. What is one step, however big or small, that you can take toward that vision?

- What opportunities open up for you if you do what is right for you? Remember, everyone is responsible for creating their own lives. Focus on creating yours, and this shines a light for others to do the same.

Whether you are in an existing relationship or in a new relationship, as you practice expressing your newly identified needs and desires, notice how it feels to do so. Maybe it's the first time in your life where you have exercised your voice, and if so, be sure to celebrate your accomplishment! How does it feel? It is normal for it to feel uncomfortable because everything new feels uncomfortable at first.

Think of those favorite pair of shoes you reach for when you want comfort. Chances are they weren't as comfortable the day you brought them home from the store. Or, maybe it feels incredibly right and long overdue! Notice the feelings and know they too offer great information. They are casting light on where you are on your journey.

As you live your life with more awareness, you might look at the happenings in your day in a different way. Has an experience showed up to create an opportunity for you to practice the new way you want to show up? Maybe an experience presents itself and serves as a test to see if you will fall back into old patterns. Practicing and applying what you are learning is key for transitioning to a new way of being. You will see what needs to be tweaked and where there is more work to do. It takes time to replace faulty beliefs and their corresponding actions that no longer serve you with beliefs and actions that do serve you. With awareness and practice, doing what feels right for you will become your new default response. Each step along the way will bring great information to shine light on what you need to do next, where your next learning is, where your next piece of healing lies. Remember, embrace the learning and let go of any judgment, criticism, or blame. Life is a series of experiences that give you the information you need to live your best life. From this day forward may you look at the moments when your buttons are pushed as containing great information and the opportunity to connect with your intuition.

Trusting your intuition and making changes take time and the more you can be gentle with the process and grateful for any and all steps you take, the more success you will experience. You might begin by introducing yourself to your intuition. Say, "It's been a long time. It's so nice to be in touch with you again." **Befriend your intuition and ask it to be patient with you as you get to know it again. Thank your body for its wisdom. Wherever you are on your path of self-discovery, be grateful.**

Place 6

Do I Really Have A Choice?

"When we look at the experiences in our lives as great information and take actions steps in the direction we desire to go, we feel empowered and are in the driver's seat of our lives. What are you programming into your GPS?"

~ Paula Anstett

Look at the following sentence and tell me what the key word is, "There are several factors that contribute to the life I create for myself." What word do you think I am referring to? I am referring to the word, "I." **You are the creator of your life. Sometimes you are a co-creator, but you are still a part of the creation. You make choices. You decide how you are going to look at the events in your life. You decide how you are going to perceive your weaknesses and your strengths. You decide if they are weaknesses or strengths. You decide how to respond.** Depending on the nature of things that have happened to you, you might resist the idea that you had any choice in the matter, but this belief can render you powerless. If you decide to take responsibility for your life and look at the events of your life through this lens, it is likely you will see where you did have some choice. Sometimes you really have to dig and peel back the layers, but if you look deep enough, you will find a place when you said yes or no and thus contributed to the trajectory of your life. I've heard people say, "I had no choice. I was given an ultimatum or threatened." Even in these moments, choices are made, and our thoughts and beliefs are at the root of what we agree or agree not to do. A single response can lead to a series of responses that seem relatively harmless in the moment and maybe even safe when independent of one another, but cumulatively, they lead you to a place that may not serve you long term. Or, maybe it does serve you for a while, and then you grow and develop in such a way that the way you are living no longer serves you.

Do you ever look at the choices before you and feel like none of them are very appealing and you wish there were more choices on your options list? Even in such situations, you still have a choice, and during such times, big picture thinking is often required. I like using a house as a metaphor. If your house has been neglected, you may need to roll up your sleeves and do some picking up, scrubbing, and grunt work before you get to do the more enjoyable pieces like painting, arranging furniture, and decorating. You have to clean up and out first if it is dirty and full of garbage. And there is no short cut. The length of time and the amount of work required depends on how long your home has been neglected. It might take time, sacrifice, and work, but ultimately the choice remains yours. Putting a reasonable plan together can set you up for success. Maybe you commit to doing one thing each day. Maybe you start by stopping: stop saying yes to what doesn't feel right and start saying no instead. Using the house as the example, stop bringing things into your home, especially things you don't want, you don't like and that do not serve you, and one by one, take out the pieces you don't want or like.

Knowing what you want and where you want to go will help you make better choices, especially when the choices before you don't seem too appealing. Where do you want to be? What do you want your life to look and feel like? Keep this vision in your mind. With an intentional and strategic approach, you will eventually come upon a time when your option's list is filled with more appealing choices.

It also makes your current choices more appealing because they are necessary to get you to where you want to be.

Remember, there is no value in criticizing previous choices. There is tremendous value in recognizing and honoring that you did the best you could at the time with the information you had, and now you are making new choices based on the information and awareness you have today. Can you see how in the years to come, the choices you make today may no longer serve you, and new ones will be required for you to achieve your new desires? Does this help you to be gentler on yourself about your past choices? Today you are making the best choice possible - one that feels right for you. You did the same thing with previous choices. Your experiences teach, grow, and prepare you for your next experiences. It would be wonderful to live life in reverse with all the knowledge you need, but that's not the way it works!

Open Your Journal

- What is something you wish was different than it currently is?

- Describe how you would you like it to be, look, and feel?

- What is something you will choose to stop doing because it will help you move toward the life you desire?

- What is something you can start doing even if it seems very small? Do you need to clear and / or create a physical space? Do you need to look at something differently and therefore let go of a mental thought pattern or a belief that is getting in the way? Write down anything that comes to mind.

Owning where you are in your life and seeing how you made choices along the way is a kind and gentle way to move through life and it empowers you to make new choices in any given moment. If you still believe you had no choice in the past, then you will likely feel as though you have little choice now. I would much rather own my past choices and have the opportunity to make new ones today than be imprisoned for the rest of my life because I continue to buy into the belief that life happens to me and I have no choice. For example, if your house is a mess and all you do is complain about it, does it ever get cleaned up? If you are waiting for a cleaning lady to magically show up and do the work for you (this is right up there with buying a lottery ticket to solve your financial problems), do you ever stand a chance of living in a beautiful, clean home? In my virtual home, I can picture the windows open and a beautiful breeze gently blowing through the windows.

Even if you are blessed to have a cleaning person show up, they only clean the surface. They don't clean out the closets. Surface cleaning will not create the ultimate life you desire. You need to clean the closets for this life to be revealed. Are you ready to roll up your sleeves? It's your life and the scrub brush, broom, and garbage bags need to be in your hands.

So, you are ready to take responsibility for where your life is going. Congratulations! This is choice number one! Now, ask yourself what you want your life to look and feel like. It may take some pondering and time for the answer to surface because many of you shut down or quieted the voice within years ago. Many people's dreams and desires have been forgotten or put at the back of the highest shelf, never to be seen again or even periodically dusted off. You bought into the belief you couldn't have them, you weren't worthy of them, or they simply weren't attainable. In essence, you bought into someone else's beliefs about what your life should be. If your dreams and desires have been shelved for a long time, it might take some time for the answers to the following questions to come: *What do I want? What would feel right for me?* This journal exercise will hopefully awaken your dreams and desires.

Open Your Journal

- Close your eyes and take a few deep breaths. Breathe into the count of four, hold your breath for the count of four and release it to the count of four. Repeat three or more times. Put your pen on the paper and allow it to write whatever comes to it. Finish the sentence: "I would love to feel…" or, "In my perfect world, a wonderful day would…" Let your pen flow.

The longer you have silenced your inner desires, the deeper they will be buried. When you remain open to the possibility of having a day that looks and feels right for you, the answers will come. Opening up to them is the first step as the answers often come when you least expect it. You might notice something in a store window that catches your eye. You might witness a couple share a kiss on a street corner and love the feeling it stirs within your heart. Your body is talking to you! Before saying you can't have whatever feeling is surfacing, express gratitude for the experience you just had and to the voice within that is waking up. When the voice is heard and acknowledged, it will speak more!

When the answers start coming, ask yourself if you are ready and willing to make choices that honor your desires. In short, this means saying yes to what feels right and no to what does not. Know that honoring yourself can be done in a kind and gentle way. You do not have to be a bull in a china shop to honor your desires. I tried this approach and realized it was part of my learning journey.

Have you ever heard the saying, *"You can't get there from here?"* As you embark toward this new destination, you might start feeling as though you are living proof of this saying. Remember it is a process. You are tuning into what feels right and the shifts you need to make. You are seeing the cleaning up that needs to take place in preparation. And, there are no shortcuts for anyone. The length of time and the amount of work required depends on how long you have neglected your "home." It might take time, sacrifice, and work, but ultimately the choice remains yours. Putting a reasonable plan together can set you up for success. Committing to doing one thing, regardless of how big or small, each day will move you along the path. A year is going to pass whether you do the work or not. Will you have a cleaner home or a messier home? Life isn't stagnant, so you are either moving forward or backward. It's an illusion to think you are staying in the same spot.

I think a home is a wonderful analogy and metaphor. What do you bring into your internal home that doesn't feel right? Are you ready to say no to anything that doesn't feel right? Are you willing to say yes to what does feel right? If this feels too overwhelming because there are so many things you need to say no or yes to, then pick one and focus on it. As the old saying goes, *"Rome wasn't built in a day."*

Before any action steps can be taken, you have to be willing to take responsibility for the changes and life you desire. For some people, this is the first step to explore and work through.

Open Your Journal

- Write, "I am willing to take responsibility for creating the life I desire!" Now read it out loud. How does it feel? Does it excite you or do you feel resistance?

- If you felt resistance keep writing and finish the following sentence, "I resist taking full responsibility to create the life I desire because…" or "I'm afraid to take full responsibility to create the life I desire because…"

It's important to identify if you are all in or if something is holding you back. If you are all in, begin making a list of things you can do to move you toward something you desire. If you are resistant, your first step is to understand what is behind the resistance. Sit with it. Visualize taking full responsibility and notice what comes. You might see something or hear words spoken by you or someone else that bring some insight.

What you choose to think in any particular moment shapes your life more than you might realize. Sometimes life sure does deal you some crazy cards, but you are the one attaching meaning, feeling, and interpretation to them. Do you feel you deserve the cards you were dealt? For many people who have experienced incredulous events in their lives, they can now look back and see how the experience was essential for them to fulfill their life purpose. Your thoughts and perspective on life are conscious choices. Are you ready to choose a way of thinking that empowers you?

To create the life we desire, we need to be in the driver's seat with our hands on the steering wheel. We need to be driving the bus, so to speak. Are you ready to drive your bus? Or are the passengers on your bus really the ones determining where your bus is going? **Can you see that there is always a choice? To create the life you desire, you must see that you always have choice, and you must be ready and willing to own and exercise your right to choose. Taking responsibility for your life is a choice.**

Place 7

Taking Responsibility
Is A Choice

"What someone says tells me where they are at. How I respond tells me where I am at."
~ Paula Anstett

Hopefully, you are ready to take responsibility for your choices and your life. It can also be called owning it. The beliefs you hold allow you to create stories about your life. What are the stories you tell about yourself to others? Listen to yourself when you are in conversation and see if you speak any words that deflect responsibility. It is important to hear what you are saying, for it offers many clues. Often, you are completely unaware of the language you use and the stories you are telling yourself and others. They reside at an unconscious level and seem perfectly normal to you. Listen for key phrases that disempower you such as, "I couldn't help it," If only," "It wasn't my fault," "The traffic was heavy," "I didn't want to upset him," "I didn't think it was a big deal," "That's just the way it goes," "What right do I have?" The list could go on, but you get the idea.

This is a valuable exercise because your language and old stories have a powerful hold on you. Quite often, their hold will override your commitment to take responsibility because you get into a push-pull situation with your subconscious and your desire for change.

When you bring whatever has a grip on you into your awareness, making changes is a different experience. Instead of using force and willpower to change, you can recognize what is at work, acknowledge it, and make a conscious decision to respond differently. Your subconscious is strong and will override good intentions if there is a lack of awareness about what is going on. Have you ever been in a conversation with someone and they are desperately trying to prove a point, but you are resisting it? What happens? Typically, they keep talking with the goal of getting you to see it their way. Sometimes they even talk louder. Notice what happens as soon as you say, "I see what you mean." Note that you didn't say you agree with them, you simply said you can see their point of view. As soon as you hear them and they feel heard, they stop badgering you. The same holds true with the subconscious mind and an old belief that wants you to keep doing what you used to do even if it no longer serves you. It keeps talking. Acknowledge it, and it will stop. You might even want to say out loud, "Thank you. I see and hear you and for a long time what you are saying worked for me, but it doesn't any longer. This is what feels right for me now." It might seem crazy, but acknowledging the monkey chatter as I refer to it, seems to work.

At the very least, it quiets the chatter allowing you to flow with the process more easily versus using force or willpower which never produces long lasting change. Willpower is about force and control - when you are using willpower to achieve a goal, you will eventually get tired, give up and go back to old ways. Remember, making changes is like training a new muscle. It takes awareness, consistent effort, and repetition. Eventually, muscle memory is developed. Now and then, old patterns will attempt to sneak back in, but with your new awareness, you can nip them in the bud. As they show up, you can say, *Oh, I see what is going on here. Thanks, but this is my new story, so what I am doing is right. Thanks for checking in. I got this.* Sometimes when the chatter is persistent I say, *You can say something encouraging, or you can sit down and be quiet. You decide.* Have some fun with it! Flow versus force - a much nicer way to go through the day. It's also less exhausting, more honoring and creates the opportunity for long term transition and change.

Open Your Journal

- Close your eyes and think of something that did not go the way you had hoped or intended. Notice what your thoughts are about it and write down what comes to you.

- Imagine telling someone else about the event. Notice the language you use when describing the situation or event. Write any disempowering words you hear. For example, "no choice," "couldn't," or blaming words, etc.

- Notice if you blamed someone or something outside of yourself for the outcome. Note: the weather and traffic get blamed for a lot of things.

- What does it feel like when you acknowledge that you actually did make a choice?

- What would it feel like for you to make a choice that better served you?

- What will you do the next time to create a different outcome? How can you own it?

- What new beliefs do you need to develop so you can take responsibility?

- Write an affirmation to reflect a new belief(s) and how you want to respond moving forward.

Even when you are feeling pressured or feel as though you have no choice, you are still the one saying yes or no. Long before I read Jack Canfield's *The Success Principles*, I believed in the value of taking responsibility for all that happened in my life. I believed I was a co-creator of my life which meant I had a contributing role in all that happened. The first chapter of Jack Canfield's book really drove home the depth of this belief, and it also highlighted that while I had control over my decisions, actions, and reactions, I did not have control over the decisions, actions, and reactions of others. Going back to the analogy of driving the bus, if you are going to hand the steering wheel to someone else, you better be ready to go where their beliefs and unhealed wounds are taking them.

I spent many valuable years taking responsibility for my life and believing that I could get the outcome I desired from others if I could get them to see my point and/or think as I did. Wrong. If I am responsible for my life, then each person is responsible for their life. If a person wants to see things as I do, that is up to them, and it is their choice, not mine. So, let me save you some valuable time. You might be ready to take responsibility for your life, but it doesn't mean the people in your life will see things as you do or are ready to take responsibility for their lives. Each person has their own work to do in this lifetime, and it will only happen if they, not you, are ready and willing to do it. They can't be doing it for any other reason than their own internal desire. For some, the fear is too significant, and they will maintain the status quo versus strive for the great, but to me, the great is living life freely, without fear. **So, get out the biggest mirror you can find and begin working on the person you see. Seek what makes you tick. Learn about the beliefs that are running your life. Become the best version of you. It is the greatest thing you can do for yourself, and for those in your life.**

The current culture focuses on seeking things externally as a means of feeling better about what is going on within. All you have to do is notice the bombardment of advertising telling you what you need to do to look better, feel better, be more successful, more popular, etc. to understand this point. With a steady drip of "this will make me feel better" going into your subconscious at alarmingly early ages, it makes sense that this is a belief that influences your adult life and your relationships. You might think, *If this happened, it would be better, or if he or she did this, it would be better, or if I gained / lost weight, toned up, it would be better, or perhaps if I got this job, it would be better.* Couples might think, *If we did this, it would be better, or if we lived here, had this, it would be better.* You get the idea. All of this has you looking outside of yourself. It also has the person you are trying to change or influence looking outside of himself or herself too. What is going on inside? Is anyone looking there?

My attempts to change the world around me and others was exhausting, held no guarantee or hope for success, and left me feeling frustrated and eventually, defeated. Finally, I learned the feeling I desired to have and the place I desired to be at required a journey inward, a journey to the self. I began looking inward, examining how I contributed to the situations and relationships in my life, what I was going to do moving forward, what I needed, what I wanted, and what I was willing to do or not do. A simple pivot that shifted my focus from outward to inward, dramatically increased my success rate and has led to a rich, fulfilling, and exciting life. Additionally, it completely changed my energy and my mindset. Instead of my days being filled with feelings of disappointment, anger and hurt, I started feeling empowered, hopeful, energized, motivated and excited. What a difference one pivot made! It was a choice to decide to look within. It was a choice to embrace a mindset to own my life and take complete responsibility for it.

Do you see potential in others and want them to reach for the stars and achieve what you feel is possible for them? Are you doing that hoping they will take you with them? Maybe you need to lead the way! Along my journey, I gave thought to why I thought I had the answers for someone else. How could I possibly know what is right for another person? At the core, this is judgment. Do you see it as judgment? I didn't either, but it is. I began noticing how I could encourage others to reach for the things I desired, but I was holding back. Have you ever done that? Are you hoping they go first and hope they take you with them? A question to ask is - *Why don't you believe you can do it or have whatever it is?* If you want something more out of life, then it is your responsibility to go for it. When the focus is on someone else, it is pure projection. What you want them to do, have, or be is actually what you want to have, do, or be. Begin owning it. Begin exploring why you struggle with feeling worthy, deserving and capable. Yep, you guessed it. There are some big beliefs that are holding you back.

Make the pivot. Realize that when you focus on someone else, you are avoiding looking at yourself. If it helps, ask yourself how it feels when someone tells you what you should be doing. If you are like me, I can imagine your answer. So, why do we do it to others? If you have been conditioned to look outside of yourself for what you need, this applies to all feelings not just happiness. Notice when you are encouraging others to do things. Have you ever thought that you are hoping they have the courage you lack? Notice the root word of encourage. It's courage. Like the Tin Man in *The Wizard of Oz*, you are looking outside for something that lies deep within. Your work is to peel back the layers and explore the beliefs you believe are lacking within, which as a result, have you seeking them in others. Being a positive, encouraging, and supportive person might hold great information, and maybe it is a socially acceptable disguise! What are you encouraging someone to do? What are you criticizing someone for not doing? Can you see both as judgments? I didn't either. But, who are you really judging? Yourself. If you are suggesting that the way someone is living their life is wrong or not good enough, whose life are you really talking about? Yours. **Take full responsibility. Look within instead of externally. Your life is yours to create and live.** Others have the same right and responsibility. Their life is theirs to create and live. Remember, you have had some pretty strong conditioning and years of practice to look out versus in, so there is no need for criticism. Awareness is the key to change!

To move through the place in between and to create the life you desire, which by the way, is your birthright (it is all of our birthrights to live true to our purpose and use our gifts to benefit the world), it is essential that you believe in taking complete responsibility for it and to feel worthy and deserving of the life you desire. It is worthwhile repeating that what makes your heart sing might be different from what makes someone else's heart sing. Do what is right for you. Hold the beliefs that serve you and let others do the same.

In closing, as you begin taking responsibility and owning your actions, reactions and decisions, there may be times when you feel scared or uncomfortable. Such experiences can be expected and are a normal part of the process especially if doing what is right for you and honors you is new to you. How many times have you made a choice in order to keep the peace or because you are afraid of the outcome or because you don't feel worthy of whatever it is you desire? Often, one of these thoughts lies behind the "I didn't have a choice" or blaming mindset. You can count on these same feelings surfacing even with your new awareness. Remember all that conditioning takes time and practice to dissolve. These feelings will surface, and your work is to explore them as they surface and do the healing necessary for you to move through them, and toward feelings and beliefs that better serve you.

Awareness is a fundamental component of your journey. Get into the habit of noticing what is going on within. What are you feeling? Where in your body is it surfacing? Can you feel it? Keep a journal.

Open Your Journal

- What do you hear yourself telling other people to do?

- What do you encourage and support others to do?

- What do you wish you had the courage to do?

- What belief holds you back?

Place 8

When Did Busy Become The New Norm?

"If you don't offend somebody at some point, you are not going to change anything."
~ Ellen Abernethy

I want to start this chapter with some questions to help you become aware of your level of busyness and its source.

Open Your Journal

- On a scale of 1-10, 1 being not very busy and 10 being extremely busy, how busy are you?

- Put a check mark beside the statements that feel true for you:

  - I'm really busy, but it is moving me towards a goal I feel passionate about.

  - My busyness allows me the lifestyle I desire.

  - My busyness is linked to my role as a parent or care-giver.

  - I feel like I am putting fires out all day.

  - I'm so busy, but that's my job, and it's a pay check.

  - My busyness is connected to my life's purpose.

  - The things I am doing cause me to feel energized.

  - The things I am doing leave me feeling exhausted by the end of the day.

  - I have the time I desire for the important people in my life and can give them my focused time.

A couple of years ago, I was at a funeral visitation. It is at such times when you see people you haven't seen for a while, or as the saying goes, you only see at weddings and funerals. As I moved from person to person and we exchanged the proverbial questions, "Hi, what's new?" or "Hi, how are you?" I couldn't help but notice I received the same response from each person, "Busy, you know." Though I knew the busy life well, this wasn't what I currently knew, and it was only because I made a conscious decision to step out of busy. Those who know me and know my fiery Aries personality were not surprised that I chose to have some fun with this. I decided to see how many people answered my question, "Hi, how are you?" with the answer, "Busy, you know." I decided to take it outside the funeral home and into the next few days. I was shocked.

When did "busy" become the new norm, and when did it become a badge of honor? It seemed to be a state of living that arrived as part of our initiation into adulthood when careers, home ownership, and children were added. And while many of the people I secretly surveyed fell into this category, it was apparent people without these additions also answered my question with the word, "busy" somewhere in their answer.

My curious mind went into overdrive. *When did people become so accepting of being busy? Why did people feel that if they responded with anything other than busy they would be viewed as "less than?" Did being busy serve people? What was the cost to individuals and families when people were so busy?*

Let's not confuse being busy with living on purpose. **Living on purpose occurs when you have goals, direction, purpose and you make conscious, intentional choices that result in full days. Your actions move you towards something, even if that something changes and evolves. At the end of the day, you can look at what was completed and what the next day holds for you. You are intentional and are driving the bus, as I like to refer to it not just getting through a "to do" list.** Busy, without goals, direction and purpose, can result in your day resembling a race. The goal is simply to get through the day. There is a feeling of lack of choice and no other way. And sadly, for most, quality time with oneself and others is seldom a part of the day or on the "to do" list.

I have lived both days and can tell you there is a marked difference in how you feel at the end of each. When you are intentional versus busy, there is a better chance that you will enjoy the moments, feel more fulfilled and ensure what is important to you and the important people in your life, is the priority and focus of your attention. Life doesn't wait for us, and it is sad to hear people say, "I wish I would have..."

Have you ever asked yourself where you want to be in a year from now? How about in five years from now? When was the last time you stepped out of your busy day and took inventory of your life and where you are headed?

Open Your Journal

It's time to take a few moments to do some pondering. Write whatever comes as you read the questions.

- Visualize yourself standing in your driveway or on a sidewalk in front of your home. Look down your street like you are looking forward into your life. What will it look like a year from now if you continue doing what you are doing today? What about in five years? Imagine what you might be feeling at that time.

- What do you want your life to look and feel like?

- Is what you are doing giving you the lifestyle you desire?

- If you leave this planet tomorrow, what will you regret not having done or started?

- What do you want your relationships to look and feel like?

- What experiences do you want to have? If you have children, what experiences do you want to give them?

- What do you want to feel in your heart?

- Given what you are doing, are you on the road to achieving what you desire? If not, what is one thing you can do to move yourself in that direction?

Write what comes to you. Reread the questions. Maybe one question, in particular, catches your thoughts. Stick with it and write what comes. You can answer as many or as few of them as you like. Remember, as you write, feelings and thoughts held at a subconscious level begin to rise to the surface so give yourself some time here. Take a few deep breaths and allow yourself to relax. Just begin writing. Let your pen take you where it takes you.

I'm going to reemphasize the importance of taking extra time here. Often, dreams and desires have been buried because they no longer seem to be on the options list. As such, it takes a while for them to surface. I remember feeling I had to get out of my nightmare before I could start dreaming. Maybe that is you too. If that is the case and, if what you are currently doing holds no possibility of your current life changing, be open to looking at something new. Do you feel too busy to add something into your life or feel like you have no choice? Look down your street like you are looking into your future and ask yourself what the cost of doing nothing will be. Never underestimate the power of a single step, a choice and doing what you can even if it seems small and insignificant. It is normal for busy people to move on to the next thing when in fact, what will move them forward is, sitting still. Let yourself stay here for a bit. This exercise has great value.

Still drawing a blank or feeling resistance? Read on and see if this opens up your mind.

If you are living a life of busy, you might begin to notice that you are running with your head down from sun up to sun down without ever looking up to see if you are on the path you desire to be on. When was the last time you stopped or at the very least looked up to see if you are headed in the right direction? Do you even know where you desire to go? Sounds silly, but when busy takes over, without knowing it, you may have veered away from intentional living and put yourself on the fast track to nowhere. I once heard if you don't know where you are going, any road will take you there. Do you know what you want? Do you know where you are going?

If you find it uncomfortable to think about what you want, then this is the place to start. I remember asking a woman in her sixties what her needs were. She looked at me as if I had three heads and said, "My needs? I don't have any." I found this incredibly sad and shocking. Somewhere along the line, she silenced her needs and desires and who knows at what age this took place. I couldn't help but think it contributed to the lack of excitement and passion she seemed to have for life. This woman was my mom, and to this day I find it sad that she gave so much to her family and so little to herself.

There are a variety of reasons you lose touch with what you desire. Maybe you are someone who feels you have never been clear on what you desire. If this is the case, you might find you draw a blank when it comes to answering the above questions. That's okay. Give yourself permission to dream now, to open up to your desires. They lie within you. For some of you, they will be close to the surface. For others, they might be buried. Ask yourself, *What thoughts come to mind as soon as I begin thinking about what I want?* Sit with this question, and you will hear the belief that has been driving your bus and holding you back from what you desire.

Have you ever watched the sequence of events that takes place when small children learn to share? When asked to give some or all of what they have to another child, they resist and often cry and throw a tantrum. When they finally concede, many are rewarded and receive something of equal or greater value than what they were asked to give up.

In such incidences, children learn there is enough for both. There is abundance. You don't have to lose when another person receives. In my opinion, the bigger message is you have to have before you can give. You can't share your Cheerios if your bowl is empty.

Do you believe in win-win relationships or is it your belief that if you win another person has to lose and vice versa? Does it make sense to you that it is only possible to give from a full cup? These beliefs can affect your ability and willingness to live on purpose and to do so without guilt. Remember, your best giving occurs when your cup is overflowing. How many of you got that message growing up? Here is a little test for you. How do you feel and respond when you see someone achieve a goal or have something they desire? Do you criticize them, down play the achievement, feel irritation, send begrudging congratulations or feel joy from the center of your heart? If you feel anything other than true joy, it could be a sign that you have a win-lose belief, a lack of abundance mindset or a belief that your desires are not possible. It is very difficult to be happy for others and encourage them if you feel it comes at the expense of achieving your desires or if it shines light on what you don't have and deep within wish you did. Why are your dreams and desires sitting dust-filled at the back of the highest shelf? What's your belief? Does being busy keep your mind off them or do you falsely believe you are working toward them? Awareness is the first step in change.

When you are doing what makes your heart sing and your cup is full to overflowing, you will notice you feel genuinely happy for others regardless of what they are doing. It might be something you aspire to do or the furthest thing from your mind. It won't matter. You will authentically offer support and celebrate their achievements. If you have difficulty celebrating others' successes, there is no need to criticize or judge yourself, simply let it be good information for you. What are some dreams and desires that you are denying yourself from having or working towards? Explore them.

When you give yourself permission to have and do what feels right for you, you end up serving those around you and the world at large. Your own cup must be full and overflowing to do so. To give to others, you must have something to give, so contrary to what many of you may have heard, giving to yourself first is essential. To love others, you must first learn to love yourself, and you must learn to both receive and to give. This message is seen in many places including the Bible, *"Do unto others as you would have them do unto you."* We hear a similar message every time we board an airplane. The flight attendant goes over the safety precautions before the plane takes off and one of the instructions is to ensure you put your own oxygen mask on before assisting your children and others.

What is being busy really all about? Is it in some way linked to the dreams and desires you no longer are in touch with or that are collecting dust on the back of the highest shelf? Today much of the busyness I see is the result of the extracurricular activities children participate in. What is this really all about? Busyness is a choice. What is the driving force behind your busy?

Open Your Journal

- What would it feel like to become less busy?

- If you have children and they are involved in a lot of extracurricular activities, what would it feel like if you weren't as involved? Is there a concern? At the very mention of it, what thoughts show up?

- What would it feel like to slow down and to have time on your hands?

- What would you do with the time?

To reap the benefits of the place in between it helps to be less busy and this might feel both scary and uncomfortable if busy has served to numb you or keep you from looking at your life as it currently stands. You might even feel vulnerable because busy can give us a sense of being in control. Conversely, you might welcome the permission to take a break from being busy with open arms.

It's important to pause and take the time you need to heal, sleep, regenerate and take care of yourself. It's a time for you to learn and practice self-love. It requires stepping out of busy for the sake of being busy. What can you say no to, even if it's only for a season or two? Maybe the saying, take one step back in order to take two forward has meaning. Notice the feelings within as you read these recommendations.

I took the following from the book, *Your Life is Your Message* by Eknath Ewswaran. It seemed a fitting close to this chapter:

"Once, while Mahatma Gandhi's train was pulling slowly out of the

station, a European reporter ran up to his compartment window. 'Do you have a message I can take back to my people?' he asked. It was Gandhi's day of silence, a vital respite from his demanding speaking schedule, so he didn't reply. Instead, he scrawled a few words on a scrap of paper and passed it to the reporter: My life is my message."

How you live your life is your message. How you live your life defines you. The amount you do in a day doesn't define you, your title doesn't define you, and your children's successes don't define you. How you live does, and this does not include giving at the expense of your own needs being met or living vicariously through others. Busy without intention, awareness, and purpose is unlikely to produce the fulfilling, satisfying, and well-lived life you desire. Don't run from yourself or negate the value of you and your desires. Allow yourself some time to get to know yourself, awaken your needs, your desires, your calling, and how you want to show up in your day. Listen to the voice within and ask for the courage to honor and respond to its message. Be kind and gentle with yourself in the process. You are worthy and deserving.

Place 9

Productivity And Receptivity

"Be the change you desire to see in the world."
~ Mahatma Gandhi

The culture I live in seems to honor and encourage productivity, or should I say busyness which was discussed in the last chapter. With the infiltration of technology, this belief is taken to new heights. Work emails are responded to in the middle of the night and in the early hours of the morning. People seem to be working more, or at the very least, are more preoccupied with thoughts about work today than in past decades. When you are carrying your work with you, which personal devices make possible, work and home life boundaries become blurred, and it seems harder to turn work off. While being able to work remotely has its benefits, I wonder if it increases expectations around how much a person should produce in any given day. I question how productive people really are when they are constantly turned on and seldom focused.

The more you exercise the productive side of your being, the more you shut down the creative and receptive side of your being.

It's during the quiet moments when thoughts and ideas come to you. When there is no quiet time, can this voice ever be heard? Today, many live in a society where people are constantly plugged in and turned on. Personal devices are turned off and recharged but how often do you create the time and space you need to recharge? Do you ever turn off?

What does it feel like for you when you stop? What does it feel like to be still? Can you tell the difference between your mind talking to you and your intuition? The place in between requires you to tap into receptivity. For those of you who tend to be very busy, it will take time to slow the pace, to create time and space in the day to pause, even stop. It requires managing the beliefs and monkey chatter that erupt when you allow yourself to stop. Pausing can be the greatest gift you give yourself. Some of the greatest things in life are free.

As a child, I had a paper route. I remember the bottom of my paper bag having a hole in it, not because the papers had sharp jagged edges that poked holes in the corner, but rather because when I wore my paper bag over my shoulder, it touched the ground and over time the roughness of the sidewalk wore a hole in the corner of my bag.

I had my paper route until I got a job at a nearby Dairy Queen. I was so excited to get that job. I was thirteen, soon to be fourteen. I would earn an hourly wage! At sixteen, I got a job at a grocery store. Again, I was filled with excitement about this new opportunity and higher wage. After school activities were not an option because of my part time jobs. Before the end of high school, my desire to make more money led me to take on a second part time job in the restaurant industry. From that point onward, I juggled two and sometimes three jobs at a time. My days were busy as I went from one job to another juggling school in between. I learned to be busy and productive. My productivity was reflected in my paycheck with my earnings being correlated to the number of hours I worked, and in my grades I got in school. I took this teaching and pattern of living into my adult life and somewhere along the line linked my value to my ability to produce.

Something interesting happened when I was in my mid-twenties, and I decided to let go of two of my three jobs and have only one full-time job. When I bumped into people I knew, and they asked what I was doing, and I had only one employer to report, I got an interesting response which initially irked me until I understood the root. The response I got was, "What else are you doing?" I came to realize their question wasn't intended to judge or to make me feel less than, instead their response simply reflected what I had taught them over the years. I was someone who always held two or three jobs at any given time. My work pattern of multiple jobs at one time was my norm and became the expectation of those who knew me. As such, their question was a natural one to ask.

Until I had this realization, I remember feeling angry and irritated when people asked me what else I was doing because my interpretation was that I was not doing enough. This wasn't necessarily what they were feeling. They were simply responding to what they knew of me to do, so asking, "What else are you doing?" was a natural inquisitive question with no judgment attached. The judgment was mine. The feeling of "not doing enough" which led to feeling "unworthy" was mine. All mine. Somewhere along the line, I learned that my value was linked to how much I was *doing*. And if the amount I had to do to feel valued was never detailed, then regardless of how many hours I worked or how many jobs I held, it would never feel like enough, because I didn't know what constituted enough. I felt that if I had hours left in my day, they should be filled with something I deemed productive. This meant if I was working only forty hours a week, I either needed to fill the remaining hours with activities that I viewed as productive, or I had to deal with my belief around productivity and its perceived link to my value.

It's interesting that despite this awareness, I didn't resolve and dissolve this belief. It just started wearing a different mask. Though I was only working one job, I always worked more than a forty hour work week. On the rare occasion when I did work forty hours, I filled the time with exercise, cleaning, formal education or other productive, measurable tasks. Seldom was the time spent reflecting, reading non-fiction for pleasure, hobbies, and fun. I guess none of these could be measured or deemed as a productive use of my time in my mind. I continue to work on this long-held belief to this day.

Where did that teaching come from? My dad would encourage me to slow down. "Sit for a while," he would say to me. Clearly the message to keep busy didn't come from this man who had no problem having a nap every day. My mother, on the other hand, definitely kept herself busy. I can't, in my opinion, say it was always a productive use of time, but I wonder if in her mind she couldn't give herself permission to "sit for a while" or use the time for pleasure. Perhaps the act of being busy served to keep her mind occupied helping her to silence or avoid the messages that would come if she "sat for a while." Looking back, I can see how my own busyness served this purpose.

You can imagine the beliefs I had to overcome as I walked through the place in between - a place that required me to be still and stop so I could hear what would come in the stillness and feel the feelings that surfaced. A place that required me to nourish the self. A place that said no to productivity and yes to receptivity.

I had to shake the belief that my worth and value were linked to productivity. I had to look at productivity differently. In the past, it was linked to a physical act, a doing. I reframed productivity and learned how receptivity was an important component of productivity. Both had value. Embracing receptivity shifted my perspective on productivity and changed what I did to be productive. It became possible to see how seemingly non-measurable acts were valuable and could move me further in my day and in my life than acts of busyness. I developed the bravery I needed to honor the dreams and desires that began to surface. I started to see that I had a purpose in this life and it would never be realized if I didn't step out of a busyness mentality. Engaging in busy tasks with the belief that I was being productive was not leading me to a life that filled my heart with joy and self-love. In fact, the opposite was settling in: anger, resentment, sadness.

What would it feel like to pause? Can you give yourself permission to stop before life stops you? Are you someone who has run yourself ragged only to hit a wall, and in doing so, you finally get the permission you need to stop? For some, the wall is an illness or an accident requiring time off for recovery, or maybe you get fired or receive a pink slip from your employer. For some, it is the end of a relationship. Perhaps it has come to you in another way.

Years ago, I broke my wrist, and it was a painful way to give myself the time I needed to stop and reflect. I was off work and could do very little for the first couple weeks other than sit with my wrist elevated. For a person who likes to be busy, there were times when more pain came from sitting than from my wrist. Stopping was exactly what I needed at this time in my life, but because I didn't give myself permission to stop or at the very least slow down so I could reflect on what was going on in my life at the time, life had a way of making it happen for me through a broken wrist.

At the time of the accident (I believe there are no accidents) I was in a relationship, and for many months I had been searching for answers as to why it didn't feel right for me. *Why wasn't I happy?* I searched my mind for any clue that would explain the feelings within. It wasn't until I was sitting idle for hours on end that I moved beyond thinking and allowed the feelings that were buried deep within to emerge. The feelings held the answers, not the mind. The understanding I sought came, and with it, the next steps I needed to take became quite clear. If you are struggling to make sense of something, look to see if you are looking in the wrong place for the information. Your body has the answers, not your head. It was in the stopping and being receptive to the messages within that led me to my next steps. I began to see that receptivity led to a new kind of productivity; a productivity that moved me forward because it was connected to my intuition and my deepest desires. Until that time, I was stuck. Stillness was needed before movement could take place. Receptivity first, then productivity. They are like yin and yang. Both have value. Both are needed.

Before my arm was out of the cast, I chose to end the relationship. We shared a home, so it meant selling my half of it to him and physically moving out. I found a room to rent in a house across town. I took the things I could fit in my new space and stored the rest of my belongings in my parents' basement. As my dad helped me unload things from my car trunk and into the basement, he said, "You know it wouldn't be good for either one of us for you to move back here." I must say that stung a bit, but he was right. I needed to sort my stuff out and make my way in life. Running back home when life didn't work out wasn't the answer, as it would do little to help me grow as a person, and with it came a message that I couldn't make it on my own. I needed to take full responsibility and believe in my ability to overcome adversity. My dad clearly believed in me, and I feel gratitude for the strength he possessed that allowed him to say yes to my belongings and no to me. I walked on.

When permission to stop comes through a life circumstance, are you able to see the gift in the experience and see how you inadvertently co-created it? Holding this perspective can be tough. It is also extremely valuable and empowering. Do you use the "stop time" to create needed change in your life? Or do you take on a victim role and miss the gift that comes on the wings of the experience? If you are reading this book, I'm thinking you are someone who is ready to pause, reflect, receive, own, and take responsibility for your life and act upon the messages that come. You are ready to say to society, "I'm redefining productivity or at the very least ensuring I include its counterpart, receptivity."

Recently a glossy magazine came to my door titled, *Women of Merit*. It was recognizing and honoring women in my community and their professional and personal achievements. Each woman was interviewed, and Q&A's filled two glossy pages along with a "Day in the Life of..." For most, their days started at 6am or earlier, and it became apparent by the end of the magazine that I should be in awe of these women who raced through their days, juggled family and careers, fit a ridiculous amount into each day, and still looked like models in the photo. Really? It caused me to remember a time in my life when my feet hit the floor at 4am, and I didn't stop until I could no longer stay awake at night. I certainly got a lot done each day, but I wasn't living the life I desired, nor was I moving in that direction, and I was tired. Actually, I was exhausted and depleted, and I was done kidding myself to think my busy, productive days would ever create the life I desired. I stared at the women in the glossy book wondering what their days really looked and felt like. Let's remember, a photo used to be called a snapshot. It captured a split second in someone's life and not necessarily the reality of the day. When you take a snapshot and add some airbrushing, professionally done hair and makeup, any female reader might question if she is measuring up. I'm sure given what I once did, I too could have met the criteria to be featured in this magazine. Knowing the reality of what such a day felt like for me, I found myself wondering what the lives of the featured women were like on a daily basis and more importantly, what did these women feel when their heads hit the pillow at night or when their alarm clock sounded in the morning.

Busyness happens for different reasons: need, transition, beliefs, and unconsciousness. Maybe for me, my snowball to busyness got rolling when I had a paper route. What I know now is that being busy does not define me. Busy wasn't fun, and it was causing me to miss a lot of important things. Without clarity, being busy didn't help me move forward, and from what I observed in my secret experiment, other individuals seemed to be on the same busy path which could lead to exhaustion and burnout, instead of desires and happiness. I wonder how many people and families would benefit if they were less busy and if "busy" stopped being a badge of honor.

Open Your Journal

- Reflect back on your childhood, what messages did you get about what your days should look like? What did you hear if you weren't doing something?

- Reflecting on what you heard, is there a link to how you currently live?

- If others perceive you based on the patterns that have become your norm, what is the current perception they might have?

- Does this way of living still work for you?

- If not, what would feel better moving forward?

- What is one step you can take toward creating a new way of living that feels better for you? If you are someone who answers, "Busy, you know," when you are asked, "How are you?" what is one thing you can say no to so you can begin the process of "un-busying" yourself?

If what you are doing is working for you, then I encourage you to continue on. In my own life, busy was no longer working for me. When I looked at my life and the lives of many around me, I wasn't witnessing too many joy-filled people. I saw people paying lip service to the people in their lives including their spouses and children. They weren't really listening. I was able to recognize it because I did it too. I'd ask someone how they were and notice I would be thinking about something I had to do for work. At dinner, I was thinking about my next day's catering menu versus asking my daughter about her day and hearing her answer.

Next time you are in a grocery store or at another place of service, notice if people are engaging with the people serving them. Or, are they talking into a microphone connected to an earpiece or typing at lightning speed on a personal device? You might think you can do two things at once, but the reality is you cannot. If you are typing, you are not listening. Period. I am seeing people who fall asleep as soon as they stop (I lived that life for years!). I am seeing people become irate when a traffic light turns red. People share what they say when their alarm clocks go off in the morning. The words certainly don't reflect gratitude and excitement for the day that lies ahead. And when I ask people how they are, the common answer continues to be, "Busy, you know." **When did busy become the new norm?** If you can identify with any of the above, maybe you are too busy.

A side note is required here. Some people who are very busy are busy because they have identified where they want to be and what they have to do to make the transition. When making deliberate transitions, life can get even busier before it gets better. There is a different intention and mindfulness around this type of busyness. I lived this busyness and can say that while it was a crazy time in my life, there was excitement and hope that came with knowing what I was doing was moving me to a better place and it was this knowing that gave me the energy and positivity I needed to put in such long days. I kept my eye on the prize and kept focused and committed. This busyness was worth every minute. Busyness with purpose, and not for the sake of being busy or keeping you from thinking and feeling about what you truly desire in life is a completely different kind of busyness. Times of transition can add busyness, so it is important to consider what you can give up during this time and what supports you can bring in to help you.

I want to give a shout out here to several people in my life who have chosen to step away from the busy, productive paradigm. They are treasured mentors who shine light on what a life of "less busy" looks and feels like. They are my beacons. They show me and others a different way of living; they show me that despite a strong cultural influence to live a life of busyness, there is a choice. I feel their support and encouragement as I continue taking steps onto paths that allow me to live differently and more in alignment with my spirit. It takes time to journey away from "what is" and towards "what you desire." Getting clear on what you desire, how you want your day to look and feel and developing the worthiness to have that which feels right for you takes time. It takes time to build the courage, time to develop the belief in yourself and time to forgive and heal, so you can allow love and wonder into your life. This is time well spent. In my mind, this is a productive use of time.

Are you thinking, *Where do I begin?* **There is no doubt that making changes can feel overwhelming. Start by shifting your thinking. Then, get clear on what you desire. No apologizing, down playing, or making justifications. Create the vision. Then, commit to taking a single step toward what you desire each day and trust there is value in the smallest of steps, especially when they happen daily.** Big or small, the steps add up. More importantly, over time new beliefs develop and strengthen, and they guide your thoughts and actions. Our thoughts are linked to our beliefs, and our beliefs are linked to our actions. This is why noticing and changing your thoughts is the place to start. Over time and distance, as your thoughts change, so will your beliefs, and your actions will follow suit. You will find it easier to say no to what doesn't feel right and yes to what does.

Open Your Journal

- Sit quietly and get a visual of what you desire and create an affirmation. Put it on the back of your business card and carry it with you. Write it on a few more cards and put these cards in places you frequent, like in the cup holder of your car, on your bathroom mirror (whiteboard markers work great!) and above your kitchen sink. Read it as many times as possible throughout your day. Developing a new thought is like training a new muscle. It takes time and repetition.

- If you are in a place of transition and know your busyness is short term, what can you say no to for the time being? What can you delegate?

I began to see that my life wouldn't crumble if I slowed down. In fact, the opposite happened. The life I desired could be built. Living on purpose does not always mean the absence of busyness, but it is a busyness that honors you and fills your cup versus draining it. That kind of busyness I can handle. For some of you, a slower pace might become your new preferred way of living. What is important, however, is to become aware of what you truly desire and what feels right for you. Then, allow those feelings versus fear-filled feelings or the expectations of others be your guide.

The place in between brings awareness to the life you are living and how it came to be. It makes you aware of the changes you desire and why you desire them and brings with it the recognition that change begins in the mind. Pausing creates the space to receive and hear your inner wisdom and desires.

Are you ready to see things differently? Are you ready to let go of beliefs and ways of living that no longer serve you? Are you ready to set new sails and in doing so chart a different course for yourself and for the generations to come? Remember, things happen when you take a single step in the direction you desire to go... and then take another. **If you want something different in life, then you have to do something different, and you can start today.**

Place 10

Why Do We Numb Ourselves?

"To heal it, you have to feel it."
~ Ellen Abernethy

Sometimes, while traveling through the place in between, the pain is so significant it can feel unbearable. During such times, it is normal, and maybe even self-preserving, to look for ways to ease it in some way or to numb it as I sometimes refer to it. As you do the inner work required to move through this space and towards the life you desire, there are times when it can feel overwhelming, and you might begin to question the healing process - if it is worth it, and if it really is possible to create a new way of living. Give yourself permission to take a break. Internal work is some of the hardest work you will do in your lifetime. In every area of your life, work is followed by rest. The same holds true when you are doing internal work and emotional processing. It is unrealistic and non-productive to be in a constant state of work without adding rest, processing, adaptation, and recuperation time. This holds true in your careers, exercise regimes, projects, and even with parenting, so it makes sense that it also holds true when you are processing emotions.

When you allow yourself to feel, the feelings can be so intense and significant, and it can feel scary and painful. You are tapping into a part of yourself that has been shut down and silenced. Picture yourself having an emotional center within, and there has been a plug on it. Most of you were not taught to express yourselves freely and honor your feelings. If your parents weren't taught the value of expressing emotions, they couldn't offer it to you. As such, the plug got put in and has remained in place for years, maybe even decades and very possibly, generations. Perhaps, over the years, there have been incidents in your life that caused you to shove the plug in further. The reservoir of emotion continues to fill up, and the plug becomes tighter with each passing generation that continues the pattern of silencing feelings and emotions. When you begin to access and release your emotions, quite naturally the feelings experienced are intense, foreign and maybe even scary. Like a held back spring once it has been tapped, the release can be significant and seem uncontrollable. It's okay, and you are okay. Trust that if you find yourself in this place, you are ready to pull the plug. Learning how to set yourself up for success can make the difference between staying with the process or giving up. To have a successful transition, you must relearn how to feel, express and release the emotions that come to surface. As a baby, you sure knew how to express your feelings, and it's time to reconnect with that instinct and willingness to feel and express.

As you allow the release of emotions and experience the feelings that come with them, I encourage you to notice how the feelings show up in various areas of your body in addition to your heart. Open up to feeling things you have never felt before, and in ways you haven't experienced before. See it as getting to know you. It might help you embrace the process instead of fearing it. If you have silenced your inner voice for a long time, it has a lot to say! Get curious and see the experience as bringing good information.

One morning while I was lying in bed, I noticed a feeling beginning to surface, and to me, it felt like grief. I was feeling it in my heart. I had been learning about allowing feelings to come and to feel them fully so they could be released. I saw an opportunity to practice what I was learning. I did a quick scan of my day and realized I had the time to try out what I was learning, and I allowed the feeling to come. I had no idea what was going to happen. The ache started in my heart. I felt it physically and remember pressing on my heart to ease the pain like you would press on an open wound to stop the bleeding. In first aid, I learned to apply pressure to wounds, so it was an automatic response to do the same with my aching heart. Interestingly, even though the wound was not open, applying pressure seemed to help lighten it. It allowed me to stay with the sensation. There were moments when I was tempted to jump out of bed believing it would stop the pain I was feeling. The act of "doing" would take over and the act of "feeling" would be suppressed. I didn't want to suppress my feelings any longer, so I chose to stay with it. I was learning that there was benefit in letting the emotion come to the surface and allowing myself to feel it. *Let it come,* I thought. *I'm ready.* I wondered what would happen. I decided to relax into it, the same way I learned to relax into a contraction when I was giving birth. Instead of resisting it, I relaxed into it. Instead of being afraid, I trusted. I allowed myself to feel it and noticed how the feeling traveled through me like a ball of energy. It began to move down my body, and I winced as I felt its presence in the different areas it visited.

At times, I wanted to do something to stop it. It was uncomfortable. I stayed with it and resisted the temptation to jump out of bed. More than once I wanted to jump out of bed and stop the process I had engaged. Then, the most amazing thing happened. I felt it travel down through my legs and straight out my feet. After its exit, I felt relief, I was calm, and my body went limp. It was the most amazing experience. I lay there in silence enjoying the relaxed state that came. I didn't realize how much tension I was holding onto and how constricted my body was. It had become my normal state after years of holding in my feelings.

As I went into my day after this experience, I noticed a new feeling come to the surface. The feeling was one of courage. It reminded me of a quote I read by Nancy Anderson, *"Courage is not the absence of fear, rather it is the ability to take action in the face of fear."* I definitely pushed through fear-filled feelings that morning. I didn't know what I was going to experience or what the outcome would be, but I dug deep and found the courage and trust I needed. It didn't kill me or cause any adverse reaction that would be detrimental to me. Instead, I was rewarded. It brought relief. The outcome reinforced the importance of befriending and trusting my inner wisdom and my feelings and allowing for their expression. From that day forward, I view my feelings in an entirely new way and allow for their expression.

I had another such experience, but this time the feeling that surfaced was anger. Actually, it is probably better defined as rage. I was in my office, and the filing drawer cabinet was stuck. Not a big deal, right? Well, on this particular day, it lit a repressed inferno within. I felt like I was going to explode and I guess that is what happens when you keep a cap on something long enough. Eventually, no amount of pressure can keep it in place. Picture a dam that can no longer hold back the water. Well, let's just say, my dam burst that day. Again, I did a quick scan of the day and saw that I could take whatever time I needed (thanks to saying no to busy!), and I seized the opportunity to let it go. I went into a nearby bedroom, and I screamed, cried, flailed and pounded the mattress until there was nothing left inside. I was spent and lay like a limp blanket on the floor. All I could hear was the sound of my breath and whimpers, and all I could feel was relief. How much are you holding onto? How much are you pushing down? It truly is amazing how much we are capable of holding onto before the dam bursts. Next time you feel agitated by something that really doesn't seem like a big deal, give yourself permission to go there and fully feel it. Let the dam break, let the emotion spill out, and do whatever you need to do to wring out every last piece of it. Yeah, it's not always pretty, and that is okay. Afterward, take a deep breath, have a shower and know that you are waking up.

I have a virtual bag of nuggets, as I refer to them, that I have been collecting over the years and carry with me to use in my life. This was definitely a nugget to pop into my bag. My collection of nuggets (life's teachings) are the tools I use to navigate my life. Just as carpenters have tools which help them work efficiently, my nuggets help me navigate the occurrences in my day. I'm sure you have heard the expression, *"When you have the right tool, the job is easy."* Most of my nuggets came from looking at situations and finding the gift. The gift, or nugget, is what I learned from the experience. I learned the value of pushing through my fears and allowing feelings to be experienced, expressed and released. I learned that it brings healing and healing sets me free. What a great nugget.

Feelings are neither good or bad, they simply are what they are. Instead of collecting them and holding onto them like a stamp collection, they need to be felt, expressed and released. They need to flow through you. They don't pay rent, so don't let them reside within you. Holding onto your feelings brings more pain, not relief, and it affects how you move forward in your life. If your buttons are easily pushed, if you regularly feel anger, frustration, irritation or sadness, if you withdraw from situations or attempt to control situations, these can all be signs that there are feelings held deep within that have yet to be felt, expressed, released and healed. Notice how your day flows. Notice what you are doing or not doing. See the value in noticing what you are feeling versus what you are thinking and then what it feels like to feel it fully and express it versus pushing it down, turning away from it or ignoring it.

Open Your Journal

- What did you learn about feelings and emotions growing up?

- What happened when you were excited?

- What happened when you were angry?

- What happened when you were sad?

- Were you allowed to express what you were feeling?

- What forms of expression were deemed okay? What forms of expression were criticized or frowned upon?

- Have your experiences, and the beliefs you created because of them, caused you to label some feelings as bad and some as good? If yes, how do you label your feelings? Which feelings do you consider as good? Which do you consider as bad?

- What do you currently do when you feel emotions surfacing that make you feel uncomfortable? What would it feel like to give yourself permission to allow them to come and to feel them fully?

Is it possible for you to look at the expression of feelings and emotions as a skill? I think it offers a good comparison and can also help you be kinder to yourself if you find it difficult to express how you feel. If you never learned to tie your shoes, would you criticize yourself for not knowing how to do it? I know, some of you would! If you were never allowed to express your emotions or worse, were criticized when you did, the skill (ability) to do so never developed. I hope that helps you to avoid any tendency to criticize yourself here. Instead, ask yourself if you are ready and willing to learn a new skill.

Think of something else you learned to do, something more complicated than tying your shoes like snow skiing or something you had to learn for work. Did it happen overnight? Did it happen without falling? Frustration? Mistakes? Fear? Maybe you wanted to quit because you felt it was too hard and you would never learn it. Learning to feel and express your emotions requires the same process. There are some strategies and techniques you can learn that will be helpful. There will be times when it doesn't go the way you planned, and you will want to throw in the towel. There will be times when you think it will never work. There will be times when your expression creates friction and hurts feelings. And there will be times when you have such a positive experience that you will yearn for more. All skills take time to learn and hone, and feeling what is going on within and then allowing for its expression is no exception.

Remember, this is a process, and be gentle, kind, and compassionate with yourself along the way. When the pain you are processing is too big, sometimes you need a break from it. No one works seven days a week without exhaustion. Emotional work is harder than any physical work you will do, so do yourself a favor and recognize it is normal to need a break from it. As with other forms of work, you need time to pause, rest, regenerate and nourish yourself along the way. Processing emotions is not a "get it done" type of task. If only it was that easy.

Let's look at how you can set yourself up for success as you learn to feel and express your emotions. Coping strategies are both important and helpful, and when done mindfully, they set you up for success. They allow you to take a break versus ignore a feeling driving it deeper within. Let's look at how a particular action can serve as a coping mechanism, and how it can also serve to keep you from doing the emotional work. Being aware of intent is so important so check in with yourself and ask what your intention is.

At one point, my entire focus seemed to be on learning. I read daily, listened to audios and journaled. I was always plugged into something. I thought I was processing emotions, but in reality, my focus was on figuring things out which is very different: one takes place in your head, and the other takes place in your body. I was spending a lot of time in my head, and without realizing it, it gave me a break from feeling what was going on in my body, my heart in particular, at this time. When I was in my head, it helped me avoid the painful feelings of loss, aloneness, emptiness, and fear that quickly surfaced when I was at rest. When I was busy, even busy learning, my time and energy were spent in my head and not in my heart. I was learning but not feeling. My heart was getting a break, but my mind was on overdrive, and without knowing it, a long held coping mechanism was engaged: keeping busy.

Keeping yourself busy to take your mind off things and numb intense feelings can create a needed break for you. The feelings haven't dissipated, they are simply put on the back burner until you are ready to revisit them. When you are actively engaged in something you enjoy, it can take your mind off your feelings and other thoughts. Busyness done with such intent can serve as a form of rest and can even be rejuvenating and build the strength you need to do more inner work. To keep yourself busy as a means of preventing feelings from surfacing is something completely different.

As previously mentioned, taking action is empowering and helps you to move forward. Getting in touch with your feelings, processing emotions and taking the time to hear the messages from within requires a different kind of active process, an internal active process and the results cannot be measured in the same way you have grown accustomed to measuring your external activity. Processing emotions isn't measured in dollars, yield, numbers, or volume. Hence, thoughts of not doing enough can, and will enter your mind and attempt to lure you away from some of the most important activity you will ever do. Instead, its measurement shows up in how you talk to yourself, how you feel, how you interact with others and what your life looks like moving forward. The changes within affect your outer world so, in the end, the inner work you do will show up in your external world. You might see it in career advancements, relationships and in your finances - the areas you are taught to use as measuring sticks. Focusing on the external without looking at the internal will create limited success. No amount of external busyness will make up for the inner work that needs to be done, which is why it's important to learn to value and create time for inner activity. Often it requires letting go of outer busyness. For many of you, spending time processing emotions and inner work will be a new way of spending your time, and once you see how the inner affects the outer, it becomes easier to give yourself the permission and the time you need.

Your inner and outer work dance with one another. Both are needed. Both have value. Both depend on each other. As mentioned earlier, when you tap into long held back emotions and process them, it can be painful and overwhelming, so let's look at some strategies and techniques that can help you cope during this time and support you in the process. I call this setting yourself up for success. Failure to see the value in pausing or taking a break when needed can cause you to give up. Don't give up on yourself. Picture the child within sitting on the side of the road. Would you walk away from her and leave her behind? Don't leave yourself behind. Do you really want to go back to your old way of living? Be patient with yourself and the process and set yourself up for success by including time to heal, regenerate, and take a break when needed. **Honor what you need with awareness and compassion.**

Open Your Journal

What do you currently use as a coping strategy or escape when you are feeling stressed, overwhelmed or when the pain of your emotions is too much to bear?

- Do you reach for harmful substances like alcohol or drugs?

- Do you reach for food?

- Do you see your current ways of coping as constructive or destructive to you physically, emotionally, mentally, or spiritually?

- Does it involve criticism?

- Do you push yourself when you feel tired and long for a break?

Before you can successfully let go of harmful coping mechanisms, you have to have something to replace them with. As with everything, it starts with a decision because anyone can say they want to change. You must decide. You must be willing to learn and implement new ways of coping. It's not about being perfect, it's about taking baby steps towards habits that will better serve you and nourish you. At the core of change is the belief that you are worthy and ready to practice acts of self-love, which is what this entire book is about, so know that you are practicing self-love when you choose coping strategies and habits that nourish you.

Methods that help me nourish and regenerate are yoga, getting proper sleep, journaling, walking in the forest, and spending time with a supportive friend. Other ways include exercising, cooking, painting, playing a sport, or being out in nature in some way. These are just a few. There are copious ways to nourish and regenerate yourself. One weekend I painted a bedroom, and without realizing it, I got lost in this task. I allowed myself to paint without urgency or the feeling that it had to get done in a certain time frame. There was no pressure, just enjoyment. At the end of the weekend, I noticed how restored I felt.

How do you know if your method of escape is constructive or destructive? Ask yourself if it allows you to hold the space you are in or does it cause you to return to old practices that do not serve you? Do you criticize what you are doing? Is it harmful to you in any way: physically, emotionally, mentally, or spiritually? Does it create the opportunity to practice new ways of being, or at the very least, not act in ways that no longer serve you? If you are choosing to spend time with people, are they offering the support you need? Do they encourage your healing, your desires, and goals? How do you feel when you leave their company? If you are meeting new people, do they have the values and beliefs you aspire to have or are they similar to the people and patterns of relationship you are working on moving away from? Is what you are doing and who you are spending time with nourishing you or chipping away at your spirit? Be mindful and aware. An easy measure is to notice if you feel better afterward. Learn to say yes to people and practices that feel right and no to any that feel wrong. This might take some practice, as it is very much like strengthening a muscle. Be gentle with yourself. It does get easier with practice. You can say no and release with love. If saying yes to others means saying no to you, give thought to your choice.

Go back to the last journal exercise. Look at your coping mechanisms. Which ones nourish? Which ones don't?

Sleep, music, yoga, nature, being with a close friend, writing, reading, painting, drawing, and cooking are just a few of the ways you can nourish yourself during this delicate time. Learn to be okay spending time alone if there are no supportive and nourishing people in your circle at this time, or choose an inspiring author to spend time with at this time. Befriend the person you see in the mirror and the inner child within. She will never leave you or hurt you, and you will never feel lonely again.

Giving yourself permission to take a break is important. A big component of the journey through the place in between includes learning to listen to the self, honoring the self, and loving the self. Noticing your feelings and learning what they are communicating to you are integral parts of the process. Remember, your feelings are neither good nor bad. Trust them and get to know them. Journaling is a fantastic way to capture what you are feeling and uncover unconscious thoughts and memories.

I want to share an experience I had a few years ago that opened my mind to looking at feelings and emotional states in a new way. One afternoon, I was talking with a nutrition colleague who studied ancient healing traditions. His perspective was enlightening and his knowledge incredible. At one point in our conversation, I said to him, "Some people think I am depressed. Maybe I am depressed." I added that I have always considered myself to be in a state of grief, not depression, and now I was starting to wonder if I really was depressed. I realized grief didn't scare me, but depression did; which was why I refused to acknowledge it as a possibility.

I didn't expect to see such a huge bright smile in response to my confession. With gentleness and excitement, he said, "Ah depression. That's great. Just go there and swim around in it for a while. Let's remember." You can imagine the look of confusion that washed over me as well as a less than excited feeling at the thought of jumping into the black hole I visualized and swimming around in it.

I shared with him that I was terrified that I would fall in and that I would never be able to get out. I was witnessing this around me: people becoming depressed and then taking prescribed antidepressants that never seem to free them of the feelings of despair they experienced. I was not interested in this path because I didn't see it offering the solution I desired. I wanted to feel free and light, so I pushed away the label depression. Pushing away the label was okay. Pushing away the feelings meant I was also pushing away the opportunity for healing and being free.

He assured me that I wouldn't fall in if I allowed myself to go there and swim around in it. What he was really saying is, "Give yourself permission to feel it." He promised me that he wouldn't let me fall in. At that time, I had not yet heard the phrase, *"To heal it, you have to feel it."*

It felt right to do as he suggested, maybe because I saw few alternatives, maybe because I love to try something new, or maybe because what he said resonated with me on some level. Plus, his promise to not let me fall in, gave me the courage to go and swim in it as he suggested. Some very somber weeks followed this decision, and I gave myself permission to stay with the process. I allowed myself a lot of quiet time (let's just say my big yellow chair and I were starting to look like a solid unit). There were points during the process that I wondered if the space I was in and the feelings that came with it would ever change. It was a very somber time. I continued to stay with the feelings that came which were less than invigorating. I had very low energy and chose not to judge myself or the space I was in. I simply allowed it to be.

Being a single mom with my own business, as much as I felt compelled to do so on many days, it wasn't an option to sit all day and do nothing. I had to get out of my chair each day and function, however, daily I allowed myself significant time, more than I have done in my entire life, to sit in silence without a book in my hand and without my fingers typing at lightning speed on my laptop. I moved through my day at a much slower pace and honored that I gave all I could during this time. I had little energy to offer my physical world. I guess all the energy was being used internally.

Finally, after several weeks, I noticed the feelings within begin to shift and the heaviness I felt start to lift. This small shift in energy brought hope. My friend was right when he assured me that I wouldn't fall in without ever coming out. What an incredible learning experience, one I will forever remember, reflect on with gratitude, and always be grateful for.

Feelings need not be feared, but felt. This experience taught me that I should be more fear-filled when I choose to silence or push down my feelings, for in doing so, I will remain stuck and the feelings will remain unhealed. Your feelings are just that: feelings. They do not define you. They are simply your reaction to an experience. If that is true, does it really make sense for some feelings to be felt and others to be silenced?

Your culture, upbringing, and influences in your life contribute to the beliefs you have around what you can feel and what you cannot. Many of you have learned that some feelings are acceptable and others are not. Has anyone heard of the expression, *Boys don't cry,* or, *Be a big girl?* How about, *Suck it up*, or, *Get over it?* To deny any feeling of its expression is to silence a part of yourself. Be willing to look at all of your feelings in a new light as you journey through the place in between. Get to know the different feelings you have not just the ones you learned were acceptable. Have the courage to explore them and allow for their expression. When you express what you feel, it makes room for the next experience to come in, and this experience gets to come into a clean space. See how life changes for you when new experiences are not mixed with lingering unacknowledged feelings.

There was another wonderful offshoot that came when I allowed my feelings full expression. Insight. Sometimes I referred to it as an ah-ha moment. I was able to see and understand something in a whole new light and with a new perspective. Acknowledging and honoring my feelings was like removing a filter from which I viewed life. I began to see life differently, and these wonderful new perspectives became the fuel for me to continue to honor and respect my feelings. Now when the feelings arise that I learned I shouldn't feel, or at the very least should not show (sadness, anger, fear, frustration), I simply acknowledge that this was someone else's belief and I saw it as truth. I was taught what feelings were okay and which ones to hide. It is up to me to determine if any teaching in my life serves me and if I want to continue to live by it. With regard to my feelings, I have decided to embrace every feeling I have. I have decided to label them all as good, and I welcome the opportunity to swim around in each as they show up. Each feeling is real, they are mine, and just like the different weather systems, they are neither good nor bad. They just are. We need rain as much as we need sunshine, in fact, how would we even know what sunshine is if we didn't experience rain? We might love sunshine, but if we only had sunshine, nature would not survive. We are like nature. All feelings, like all weather systems, are valuable and needed for our survival and for us to grow and flourish.

Learning to notice and feel what you are experiencing is an important part of the healing process, a process that allows you to live your truth in peace and knowing.

As you transition from one place to another, there will be times when you will feel like running back to what was comfortable even if in reality, it wasn't comfortable at all. If it was, you wouldn't have chosen to step away from it and into the place in between. It's all part of the process. It's like doing a big renovation in your home. Mid way through it you think, *Why did I do this? What I had was fine.* You can choose to live with what is, but in doing so, you limit the exceptional experience that is possible, something which you long for deep within. When in the midst of a home renovation, the reality is, you are now in it, and there is no going back. Keeping the picture of the finished project in your vision is what keeps you going. When it comes to personal work, you can give up and go back, but can you really go back? During times when you feel this way, I encourage you to pause. Nourish yourself. Take a break. It's important to allow time for processing, healing and assimilating new thoughts and ways of being. And when it feels right, continue to walk on.

Learn to ask for and accept what you need from others. Many of you will find receiving extremely difficult. If you are one of those people, like I am, spend time pondering why it is so hard for you to receive. There will be great information that comes from your exploration. It is important for you to be able to give and receive. If you cannot receive, it is usually linked to feeling unworthy. When you can't receive, you deny others the opportunity to give. Maybe this realization will help you open to the idea of receiving.

To say no when people offer to help is to say no to the flow and abundance of the Universe, the infinite source that is bringing what you need to you. Learn to say yes. Learn to feel worthy. Learn to say, "Thank you." People who love you want to help. If you think you are weak or needy, ask where those beliefs came from because they are beliefs, not truths. You are worthy of love, support and nurturing.

There is goodness in being able to give and receive. Learn to do both. And remember, be gentle, kind and compassionate with yourself.

Open Your Journal

- Are you someone who can give freely, but have difficulty receiving? How does it feel to receive help from others?

- What is your belief about receiving?

- Is it a truth or a belief?

- How can you rewrite that belief so it better serves you and allows you to be nourished?

- List three or more ways to nourish yourself that you can use when you need a break from feeling or processing emotions and healing. Let these become ways for you to fill your cup, give you time to regenerate and prepare you for the next step.

Place 11

Nurturing The Self

"The greatest gift I can give myself is unconditional love."
~ Louise Hay

In the last chapter, we talked about coping strategies that can help us when the pain of processing emotions and healing becomes too much to bear.

Taking a break can be extremely valuable. We touched on the difference between doing something as a means of creating a diversion that will help you rejuvenate versus keeping busy for the purpose of avoiding what you need to do. The topic of productivity came up, and the focus of this chapter is to further explore your relationship with productivity and the beliefs you hold about productivity that may or may not serve you.

Close your eyes and picture yourself having a very productive day, in whatever way that looks for you. Notice what your day looks like and notice how you feel. What thoughts and feelings do you have at the end of the day? Write what comes to you in your journal.

Now close your eyes and picture a day when you did very little.

Maybe you spent the day chilling out on your sofa, reading or watching T.V. Maybe you spent the day procrastinating and didn't accomplish what you intended to do, nor did you give yourself permission to do something else. Notice what thoughts and feelings come to you at the end of this day. Write down what comes to you in your journal.

This chapter is about exploring your relationship with down time, rest and reflection time. A farmer knows the value in nourishing and replenishing the soil in which he grows his crops. If he continues to plant seeds without offering nourishment to the soil, the quality and quantity of his yield are compromised. Advancements in technology could be one reason people are in productivity mode more than rest mode. Cultural expectations and pressures could be another. There are likely many reasons, but what is important is to bring awareness to how it is affecting you. How is your current paradigm affecting your ability to process emotions, to heal, to make needed changes, to rejuvenate and gain clarity on what you desire? How has your physical, emotional, mental and spiritual health been affected if you have fallen prey to an imbalance between productivity and rest? Many people are finding that their health has been greatly compromised in one or more areas. Listen to the words people use, and you will get an idea of the impact. Words like, "depleted, tired all the time, emotional, exhausted, depressed, impatient," are all clues to the impact such a way of life is having on people.

When people reach the states listed above, rebuilding can take a significant amount of time, and it will bring to the surface your relationship with productivity and rest as well as beliefs that may not be serving you.

Open Your Journal

Simply write yes or no to the below questions.

- Do you have any quiet time in your day?

- Do you eat enough to nourish you?

- Do you eat sitting down or do you eat on the run or in your car?

- Do you get enough sleep?

- Do you participate in exercise that feels good or exercise that you feel you should do?

The above questions can help you see if you are nourishing yourself on a basic level. If these are not a part of your daily life, why? An easy answer would be that you don't have time, but I'm not going to let you off the hook that easily. What are you saying yes to that you could say no to? Can you see how saying yes means you are saying no to nourishing yourself?

Many people have picked up a belief along the way that they are not worthy, and sadly, most women I speak with hold this belief. It doesn't matter where it came from. What matters is that you get in touch with it and take steps to develop feelings of worthiness. Sometimes you trick yourself into believing you are worthy. Let's look at how that shows up.

Is there a qualifier on your act of self-care? Qualifiers can be defined as anytime you justify doing something. For example, I bought a new outfit because I put in so many extra hours at work. I took a night to myself because my husband was away all week and I was so busy running the kids around on top of everything else I do. I bought a new pair of shoes because they were on sale. I went to the gym because I need to lose some weight. The "because" is the qualifier. Can you do something simply because it felt like the right thing to do for yourself? Can you do something because it is an act of self-care? Self-care is a birthright. When did it become something you had to earn?

That's a tough one for most of us, and I would be lying if I didn't say it is an area I continue to work on. Do something or buy something because you want to. No explanation needed. No justification needed. I am worthy of things that are nourishing (physically, emotionally, mentally and spiritually) and that bring me joy.

Does self-care/nourishment happen as part of your daily and weekly regime or does it only happen when you become so depleted that you have no choice because you can't keep going? Do you have to become ill in order to put self-care on your priority list?

Open Your Journal

Answer the following questions with a yes or no.

- When you are not feeling well, do you honor your body's need to rest or do you plow on?

- Do you allow others to care for you?

- Do you accept help from others or do you say, "It's okay? I can do it."

- Do you continue to take responsibility for things that can be delegated or that are not your responsibility in the first place?

- Do you vigorously exercise at a time when your body needs rest (restoration) and gentleness?

- What do you do when you find yourself in a perpetual state of feeling tired? Do you drink more coffee? Do you criticize yourself for not getting everything done? Do you rest?

- Do you look for ways to reduce your load?

- Sleep is one of the biggest contributors to good health. Are you getting enough sleep (8 hours)?

Let's pinpoint what is taking up your time and see how a change in perspective can change what you do and how you accomplish your daily tasks.

Make a list of everything you do or as much as you can think of, in a day and over a week. Next, you are going to number them.
Put a #1 beside the things you *like* to do and *want* to do.
Put a #2 beside the things you feel you *need* to do.
Put a #3 beside the things you feel you *have* to do.

Get a highlighter and highlight the items on your "have to do" list(s) that you would love to *not have* to do. Do the same on your "need to do" list. Highlight the items you wish you *didn't need* to do. Look at both of these lists. Pick the items you can you either stop doing or delegate and write them on a separate page. This might require you to get over the belief that you are superwoman or can do it better than anyone else. You are all "super" women and let's not confuse being super with the belief that to be super you have to do all things and be all things to everyone around you. This exercise might be more challenging than it looks because it is likely to poke at your beliefs. Good! That's exactly what this entire book is about!

Do you see some items that would be easy to stop doing? Great! Pick those first. Next, look at the ones that can be delegated. Jot the name of the person who you could delegate it to beside the task. With the items that you can stop doing - write down why you are going to stop doing them as a reminder to yourself. For example, I am going to stop (fill in the blank) because it will give me a 15-minute time slot for a walk, or it will allow me to get to bed 15 minutes earlier. Add an affirmation: *"I am worthy and deserving of this nourishing time."*

Next, look at the items that require transition time. Pick one item on the list. What is required to make the transition, so you are no longer doing that item? Write down everything that needs to happen or be figured out. Number the steps and commit to taking action on step number one. Remember, if you do one thing, big or small, every day to move yourself forward, your life will look differently in a year. So, what is one thing you can do today? Maybe you need to make some calls, make some inquiries, do some research. These are valuable action steps. If you want your life to change, commit to a baby step.

Next, let's think about these three statements:

Have to… Need to… Want to…

Open Your Journal

- Close your eyes and think about something you "have to do." Notice the feeling within. Jot down what you are feeling in your journal.

- Now, close your eyes and think about something you "need to do." Notice the feeling within. Write what you are feeling in your journal.

- Lastly, close your eyes and think about the things you "want to do" and notice the feelings within. Again, describe the feeling in your journal.

Go back and read what you wrote. It is common for people to experience different feelings. Isn't it amazing how a different energy is created within you by changing just one four letter word? When you want to do something, the energy you need comes to you. When you feel you "need to" or "have to" do something, it seems to drain your energy. One nurtures you, the other two do not. How many of you feel tired simply because there are too many "need to" and "have to" situations in your day?

When I did this exercise, there was a notable difference in the feelings I experienced, the energy I felt and the mindset I had when I "wanted" to do something versus when I felt I "had" to or "needed" to do something. Remember, everything in life is a choice.

Look at your list. Are there things on the "have to" and "need to" lists that you could stop doing, delegate, or transition out of doing? The tendency is to think you have no choice. There is always a choice. If what you hear as you read this is - *What will others think?* - you know deep within that you have a choice, and it is beliefs that are fueling your decisions not desire. Maybe the words you hear go something like this, *No one else can do it, so I have to.* Is it really true that there is no one else that can do it or is the thought linked to wanting to have control or a concern about what people will think if you don't do it? Take the time to explore your current beliefs and how they serve you and others. Be completely honest.

If you feel there is absolutely no way you can stop doing something on your "need to" or "have to" list, can you think about the task differently? For example, if you are caring for a disabled or elderly person in your life or have young children who require your care, can you get some help? Can you allow others to contribute or are you someone who feels you have to be in control because you know best how to care for him or her, or maybe you are worried what others will think if you aren't there 24/7? If getting some help isn't an option right now or you really don't want someone else to be involved, can you begin saying, "I *want* to be there and care for this person?" If you don't want help, then you are saying you *want to* do it versus *have to* do it. If help is not available at this time, choosing to say you *want to*, versus *have to* or *need to* can make a marked difference in your day and in your energy. Try it out. Put want to in the sentence instead of *need to* or *have to* and notice if it changes the feeling within.

It is key to recognize that there are only twenty-four hours in a day. You are blessed when your day is filled with all the things you love to do, and yet if it is still overflowing, it is necessary to say no to something.

I close this chapter with a quote that helped me shift my perspective on taking time for myself. Rita Davenport is a motivational speaker and author. During one of her keynotes, she said, *"If you had a dollar in your pocket and I asked you for five dollars, could you give it to me?"*

This example holds true in all areas of your life not just with regards to money. If you have no time, and I ask you to listen for a moment, can you take the time to really listen? If you have no energy, and I ask you to do something for me, can you offer it? If I need your patience and understanding, but you are depleted, can you give it to me?

Learning how to say no to what does not serve you and yes to what does is a significant piece required to nurture the self. What can you say no to right now? What things could you say no to but the chatter in your mind is saying, *But what will people think?* Notice the thoughts that enter your mind. Is there truth in the thought or is it a belief you picked up along the way maybe from a parent, friend, teacher, coach or neighbor? Does it serve you today? If it doesn't, are you willing to let it go or change it? It's important to recognize what beliefs are running your life. Are your beliefs or someone else's running your life? Awareness is the first step to change.

As you know, change doesn't happen overnight. The exercise above brought forth information and awareness of the things you don't want to do and why you continue to do them. As you travel through the place in between, it becomes essential to explore your beliefs. Whose life are you living? The life you live is created by your thoughts and your beliefs. Are the thoughts and beliefs you live by really yours or are they the beliefs of your father, mother, school teacher, coach, aunt, friend, spouse / partner, or employer? Maybe they are beliefs you created based on how you interpreted an experience. If a belief serves you and aligns with the life you desire, that's wonderful. Keep it. If it doesn't, commit to letting it go and replacing it with a belief that does.

"Even if your life is crowded with the old, find the spaces to dance in."
~ Colleen Marana

Change is achievable by taking steps, sometimes very small steps, towards that which you desire. Small, gentle changes are particularly important when you have identified something you no longer want to do but you feel to stop doing it would cause too much disruption and chaos in your home, workplace, or relationship. Instead of thinking you *should* continue on so you don't rock the boat, open up to the idea of making a plan to transition to a new way of doing it, or maybe not doing it at all.

The process of loving and honoring your needs requires you to learn to say yes to what feels right and no to what does not feel right, and to feel worthy of what you desire. For me, when I first started saying yes to what felt right and no to what didn't, often there was fear and anger behind my words, and over time I learned the anger was a defense mechanism. I was afraid of being rejected, judged or yelled at if I said and did what was right for me and my angry tone created an energy around me that had most people backing away from me. I now can see how my anger served to protect me. Responding with an angry tone seldom got me what I ultimately desired, but at that time it was the only strategy I had. As I continued to work on feeling worthy and loving myself, my fear of rejection and judgment began to diminish because the most important person in my life loves me unconditionally, will never leave me, and no longer judges or criticizes me. That person is me. Developing my sense of self and love for myself gave me the courage I needed to ask for what I needed and to respond with love when people tried to pull me back into old patterns that served them not me. Responding with love, not anger, is much nicer for everyone.

Be mindful of your cup. For you to thrive and to be of service to others, including your partners and family, your cup needs to be full, ideally overflowing. **Learning to say no is key to your health. Learning to say no may seem selfish, but in truth, it is an act of self-care. You would not deny yourself food for nourishment, so why do you deny yourself rest? Both are nour-**

ishment, and both are needed by the body for survival and function. Shifting your perspective can help you say yes to what you need and no to what does not serve you at this time. It can also help you turn a task from draining your cup to filling your cup.

Place 12

Pulling The Thread

"When one tugs at a single thing in nature, he finds it attached to the rest of the world."
~ John Muir

As you move through the place in between, you will begin to feel increasingly ready to go out there and try on your new way of being. I remember being open to going on a date and in doing so, I realized I was not ready. This was simply good information and led me to the next pieces I needed to look at, work through, resolve and heal. About a year later, after more exploring and healing, I felt ready again and not only did it feel better, it actually felt right. There is no need to judge the space you are in and absolutely no value in criticizing yourself thinking you *should* be further along. The present moment is what it is, and in the end, you will see that it is a necessary part of your story. There is significant value in honoring where you are, how far you have come, how much you have achieved, and how many changes you have made since the beginning of your journey and the many steps you have taken. Being in touch with your feelings continues to be important. Sometimes knowing how to honor what you are feeling and allowing yourself to respond is not always clear, but the answer will come if you listen to your intuition and the feeling deep within versus the voice in your head. Some people call it intuition, some feel it is Spirit or God speaking to them, and some see it is their higher self. Can you tell the difference between this inner voice - your inner wisdom, and the voice in your head - your thinking brain?

Maybe it would help if instead of saying an intuitive *thought*, you said an intuitive message or an intuitive *feeling*. The messages you get from your intuition come without thought, before thought. For instance, sometimes I ask people I work with, "Who is someone you would like to talk to about your business?" Almost always, a name immediately comes to mind, and it is quickly followed by a reason to not call him / her. The name that comes without thought (in a split second) comes from your intuition. The reasons to call or not call come from the thinking brain that holds beliefs, trauma, insecurities, and memories.

When something truly feels right to you (and this feeling can lack reason), it is coming from your intuition - your inner knowing. Learn how your body talks to you. You often hear people say, "I have a gut feeling." This is their intuition talking to them. Do you ever get a gut feeling? Do you trust it and listen to it? Or do you ignore it or override it with logic? Are you in tune with how your body communicates with you? Do you believe in inner wisdom and guidance? What does it feel like for you to listen to it? If you study history, you will see that throughout it, there is a first for everything and the people who dared to honor the feelings within were often told their ideas wouldn't work. Some were even laughed at, some might have been ridiculed even ostracized for following their intuitive voice, the voice of their higher self or from God. Listening and responding to the messages from within are at the root of many extraordinary accomplishments.

Moving beyond limiting beliefs can cause feelings of anxiety. People who achieve what seems to be extraordinary are not void of feeling anxious, rather they see anxiousness as just a feeling. They notice it, they feel it, and they keep going. Pushing through when it feels right to do so is a different experience than pushing through using your mind as the force. How can you tell the difference? Often the word "should" will be in the latter. I *should* do this, or this *should* work. If the word *should* is used to override what you are feeling within, you might want to pause and look at what is driving your thoughts and actions. Is it truth or belief? If it is belief, is it your belief or someone else's?

It is important to be aware of what I call *gremlins*. Gremlins are words spoken from an inner voice, not the voice of intuition but rather the voice of old beliefs that you currently hold as truths. Gremlins show up and attempt to keep you from growing and moving forward. This voice shows up to keep you back and wants you to continue to play small in life. Gremlins are someone else's voice. Intuition is your voice. Gremlins are someone else's beliefs and feelings. Intuition comes from your innate wisdom and feelings. Note the difference between the two, and note where each comes from. Gremlins speak the words and messages you heard from the people in your past. Instead of disregarding them at the time they were spoken to you, you held onto them, and they became laws you live by. They are not truths. They are someone else's opinions, and you have chosen to see them as truths. Intuition comes from deep within your soul. Most people are unaware of the beliefs that are charting the course of their life because they reside at an unconscious level.

Let me give you an example of what I mean about beliefs and memories that reside in your unconscious and how they show up in your day. Is there a song that brings back memories for you every time you hear it? When you hear it, even the first few notes of it, you are immediately taken back to a time and place in your life. How about a smell? Have you ever caught a whiff of something and it took you right back to something your mom used to bake or cook? Scents do the same. When I smell fresh Lily of the Valley, I am immediately taken back to the house I grew up in. Senses are powerful, and they hold memories in the unconscious mind. Such occurrences happened without thought. They are memories that reside in your unconscious and are brought to life by something that happens in your present day. Do you think the unconscious only holds on to the positive memories and positive words spoken by people in your past? Wouldn't that be wonderful! It also holds onto the not so wonderful experiences and damaging words that were spoken. While the positive ones often bring warmth and a smile to your day, the negative experiences show up in your day too. You see them in the actions you take or don't take as well as in your reactions. They can show up as fears, anger or anxiety. Do you ever feel fearful and yet it seems there is no reason to feel fear? Do you ever react angrily to a situation that stirred no emotion in the person sitting beside you? Do you ever wake with anxiety, yet you know you are safe? These feelings are being triggered by a memory stored in your unconscious, and instead of it being a memory that brings warmth and allows you to move lovingly into your day, it can prevent you from taking the steps you desire to take.

Becoming aware of the different voices within can be empowering because you learn when to honor what you are hearing and when to say, *Thanks for your input. If you are going to cheer me on, great. If not, please (go and) sit down and be quiet.* This takes practice, and it can be likened to training a muscle. It takes time, and over time the muscle strengthens. Now, all I have to do is give "the look" to the gremlin (I visualize him sitting on my shoulder), and it leaves. That's progress! It's the same with your intuition. It is sending messages constantly, and you will find that life is so much easier when you welcome its guidance. Begin with the simpler messages you receive. Next time you are driving somewhere, and you get a gut feeling to take a particular route, trust it. See what happens. Maybe you get a feeling to grab your umbrella even though the sun is shining. Take it. See what happens. Who cares if it doesn't rain that day. Applaud yourself for honoring the voice within. Begin noticing the different voices within, and the interplay between them. What do you hear first? **The more you trust and honor your intuition, the more it will speak to you. Have fun with it. It might help you understand why sometimes you feel conflicted. At the very least, find comfort in knowing there is a force within you that wants you to succeed. You are not alone.**

As you learn to differentiate between your intuition and your thinking brain and build a relationship with your inner knowing, it will hopefully help you develop the courage you need to act in ways that honor your needs and desires. For some of you, this might mean doing things differently from what you have done in the past. For others, the changes might be smaller. You might test the waters by making small changes in your behaviors and actions (and quickly) only to notice that in doing so, feathers are being ruffled in many areas of your life. Why does this happen? When people are used to seeing you behave and respon in one way and then you make changes, it often means they can no longer respond in the way they have grown accustomed to. If you picture yourself in a dance, which in essence is what you are in with every person in your life, and you suddenly change a step, your dance partner is thrown off. He was expecting you to move a certain way and his next move was already planned based on this expectation. This is in essence what happens in your interactions with the people closest to you when you make even the smallest of changes. They are thrown off. What they expected didn't happen, and they might not be able to respond in their usual way. In turn, there is uncertainty, confusion and this can cause feelings of insecurity and uncertainty in some people.

Furthermore, how you show up in one area of your life is usually how you show up in all areas of your life. Hence, when you make even the smallest change in one area of your life, it is likely you will do so in other areas of your life too. If you are taking a back seat when it comes to your partner, then chances are you do the same in the workplace. Change how you interact at home and most likely you will begin interacting differently at work.

Have you ever heard someone say, "Oh my gosh, my whole world is crumbling," or, "It seems I'm at odds with everyone these days?" When you change a belief or a behavioral pattern, the change is taking place within, so it will be experienced in all areas of your life. Have you ever noticed how your relationship with a co-worker or a boss has similar components to the relationship you have with your spouse, sibling, parent, friend or child? Have you ever noticed that if you take a passive role in your family or personal relationships, often you are also passive in your work environment or in a club to which you belong? Side note: There are exceptions where people show up completely different in another area of their life. Can you see how changing a pattern of behavior at work, will also show up in how you interact at home? At the very least, you might feel some agitation because now you have new awareness and you cannot undo this.

This helps to explain why when you start the process of change, a thread is pulled through your entire life. Relationship choices, work preferences, where you live, and the friends you have all support your current way of thinking. When you start to change the way you think, you begin to see how all the players in your life have supported and brought perceived truth to your thoughts and beliefs. Remember, your thoughts and beliefs are learned. They are not truths. Becoming aware of what no longer works for you creates the opportunity to explore and develop new thoughts and beliefs that better serve you in the present moment.

In a previous chapter, I talked about how you teach people how to treat you. They are responding to how you live, and how you live is based on your belief system. In the example, I explained how I always had two or three jobs, and this is what people grew to expect. This way of working was in alignment with my belief system at that time. If I wanted people to respond differently, I had to teach them my new way. I encourage you to be gentle and compassionate when implementing new ways of being. Your new thoughts and beliefs might be met with resistance if the people you are interacting with perceive the change to have a negative impact on them. It is likely that your new way of wanting to be in these relationships will require others to change. It does not matter whether or not your current relationships are working or not, many people would prefer to keep things as they are rather than change and move into uncharted territory.

I like to use this metaphor to help explain what is taking place. You and your partner, friend or coworker have been playing the game Monopoly for years. You both love this game, and you play it every day. After years of playing it, you think to yourself, *I don't want to play this game anymore. I want to play Yahtzee*, and you pull out Yahtzee and insist on playing it. "Yahtzee?" the person exclaims, "I don't like that game. I want to keep playing Monopoly." You insist Monopoly no longer interests you and you don't want to play it anymore. If the person you are talking to is open to looking at something different and learning a new game, you are off to the races. Most times, it is not that simple. People within a relationship often prefer to keep things as they are even if it no longer serves them. They fear opening up Pandora's box, the unknown. In this example, you actually told the person you wanted to play Yahtzee instead of Monopoly. In real life, the tendency is to change the game (your way of interacting) without any warning, without any conversation about what you are feeling and why, and then expect the person to respond favorably and willingly. Developing awareness around what you need and desire is key for you to live true to yourself. Communicating your awareness is a critical step, and the players in your life deserve to know that you want and need to change the game. They aren't mind readers. Fear often holds you back from having open and honest conversations. Take the time to explore the fear. Feeling worthy is often at the core of fear-filled feelings.

Hopefully, these examples help you see why it seems feathers are being ruffled in all areas of your life when you decide to make changes. This is simply something to note and to learn to navigate. It is not a reason for you to go back to old ways that no longer serve you.

Having some awareness around how your decision to change a belief that no longer works for you can affect others in your life is important. It can help you navigate the emotions, possible discord, and fear that may surface both within yourself and within others. Some relationships move through the change process somewhat smoothly because both individuals are willing to make changes. For some, it will mean a relationship needs to end. How you view the end of a relationship (work, family, friend) will have a significant effect on your ability to move through it.

If you have learned, healed and grown from a relationship, then was it a successful relationship or a failed relationship? Notice the patterns that exist within the various relationships in your life - work, personal, and friendships. Observe how each relationship is experiencing some discord and is shifting and changing. Do you view this as your having a problem and not being able to commit or get along with people? Or do you see the pattern and acknowledge that a single belief is the culprit for the discord in each of these relationships? When you make a change in one relationship, it is like pulling a thread. It is likely that the belief you are changing can be seen in every area of your life and just like a thread holds an entire seam together, your belief or set of beliefs attracted the current people and situations in your life to you. Some of you will see this as fascinating and exciting. For others, it will feel scary. How you perceive the information will determine how you move forward.

Perspective is a fundamental component which determines how you move through life and whether you choose to see life as a collection of experiences designed to help you learn and grow, or whether you see the choices you made as right or wrong. Do you see your decisions as mistakes, or do you see them creating experiences that bring learning and usually a nugget of wisdom if you look for it? **Life is a collection of experiences. What you do with that collection is up to you.** If you believe that you make mistakes, the tendency will be to look back with regret. If you see decisions as creating experiences, the tendency will be to look forward with anticipation and excitement and you will course correct along the way. One brings negative energy. The other brings positive energy. How you view your experiences correlates to whether you cycle in patterns that no longer serve you or you choose to learn, grow, and move forward toward the amazing life that awaits you.

It takes courage to do what feels right for you and to live in a way that honors your purpose and desire. Remember, each of you has a perspective, and it is based on what you have learned, how you were raised, and new ways of thinking that you are open to considering. Sometimes a perspective is shared with you, and it resonates with you, so you let it in. Hopefully, you do so because you feel it will serve you in a positive way. Other times, someone offers a perspective that doesn't feel right, and it takes awareness and courage to say no to it. This can be a perspective about how you *should* live, where you *should* live, what you *should* take in school, who you *should* date/ marry, how you *should* dress, the list could go on. The list is infinite with the word "should" being the constant. The word "should" does not imply truth or rightness.

Remember, if you choose to do things that make sense in your head (which is linked to accepting other people's perspectives), but not in your heart, then be sure you like how they are living and where they are heading. In other words, if you choose to accept their perspective, you are also choosing to walk in their shoes. Do you like where their shoes are going?

Making one change can have a powerful ripple effect because it will be seen, felt, and experienced in all areas of your life. Notice how a pattern you change in one area of your life, shows up in another area. Be gentle with the process, yourself and with others. Feel worthy. Communicate your desires. Have compassion with how the change affects someone in your life. Validate feelings and keep moving in the direction you desire. Own what is yours and let go of what is not yours. Over time, your new way of showing up will become your new normal, one that is honoring to your spirit. **Self-awareness, self-confidence, and self-image all improve when we live in truth and honor.**

Open Your Journal

- Think about something you want to do or a change you are considering. What is the first thought that comes to you? What is the second thought you get? Notice the difference between the two.

- How would it feel to honor the first thought that comes?

- How would it feel to honor the second thought that comes?

- Can you give yourself permission to trust and honor the one that feels right versus the one that has logic behind it?

- Begin noticing the "shoulds" in your life. They often signify what you don't want to do.

Place 13

Exploring The Shoulds

"Do what you feel in your heart to be right for you'll be criticized anyway."
~ Eleanor Roosevelt

In the previous chapter, I talked about the word "should" and how it affects the choices we make. How many times is *should* at work without our awareness? The concept of *should* resides in the unconscious mind and without our awareness affects many of our actions or inactions. As I traveled through the place in between, I began to notice the various places that *should* showed up and how it directed my choices.

Here is an example of how an unconscious "should" influenced a vacation choice. Years ago, I went to Disneyland because of a work-related event, and I was grateful for the opportunity to experience a place I heard so much about and watched on television as a kid. While there were parts of it I enjoyed, most of it wasn't what I like to do or experience when I am on holiday because my preference leans more toward nature and physical activity. In addition, there were many components that didn't align with my values. There was no recycling, the waste was significant, the consumption of nonnutritious food was bothersome, and instead of seeing the magic and creative genius that one man possessed and ignited in others, I saw people seeking to quell an insatiable need for consumption whether it be with pricey trademarked souvenirs, nutrition deficient food or with fantasy and entertainment. On one hand, I admired people's ability to embrace the experience. On the other hand, I wondered what inner void were they trying to fill. I struggled with being herded like animals through a busy, hot park. A park devoid of grassland and nature and made up of cement, steel, and stimulus. My curious mind was constantly engaged.

This begs the question of why I recently chose to take my daughter to Disneyland. Somewhere deep within there was a belief that every child, every person *should* experience the wonderful world of Disney, a belief that got planted deep within my unconscious at a young age thanks to advertising. I bought into the marketing versus looking within to see if it aligned with my values and what I like to do during my vacation time. I wish I could say this realization occurred before I spent thousands of dollars, but it happened on the second day of our vacation when I was trying to convince my daughter to be excited about going to the second of the four theme parks I purchased passes for. All she wanted to do was go to the pool that was steps away from our room. All I could think of in that moment was, *This is one expensive pool.* It was her comment, "Mom, can you tell me what is fun about taking a cold bus to a park then walking all the way across a park, so we stand in line for an hour for a two-minute ride?" I could have diverted the comment by saying the ride was less than thirty seconds but that would not have helped my case. Instead, I surrendered and said, "Good point. Let's go to the pool." And the pool is where we spent most of the following five days. Ouch. When planning our holiday, I consulted the *should*, versus the opinions of those who really mattered: her and me. It was an expensive lesson and I am grateful for it because it helped me see the many other places where *should* has been at the helm of my decisions. The *should* is friends with, *What will the neighbors think?* and the next time either one shows up, I will ask them whose credit card is being used.

As I move through the place in between, I am learning to both love myself and be myself. Be who I am. Be okay with saying, "I like this. I don't like that. I want to do this. I don't want to do that." My daughter is fantastic at doing this, and I notice how sometimes her clarity and unwillingness to cooperate when things don't resonate with her ruffles my feathers. Sometimes it's because we desire to do different things, so saying yes to her means saying no to me. More often, my uneasy feelings are linked to fear. *What will her life look like if she always gets her own way? Will her perspective and experiences be too narrow if she only does things that feel right or serve her? What happens if she never learns to go outside her comfort zone?* Then I thought, *Why am I not more concerned with what her life will look like if she doesn't honor who and what she is which includes her likes and dislikes?* The "should" and "What will the neighbors think?" are powerful forces. Somewhere along the line, I learned that it was more important to fit in and do things that worked for others than it was to do what felt right for me. Is this what I want her to do? Is there a place in between? It is one thing to consciously compromise, it is another thing to never voice your desires, preferences, likes, and dislikes. If being accepted by others comes at the expense of self-acceptance, how can we expect self-esteem and self-love to be developed? It's a disconnect and isn't a lack of self-esteem and self-love at the core of many challenges people face?

As you move through the place in between, you learn so much about yourself. You become stronger, begin to acknowledge and accept who you are, and love yourself for who and what you are. It would be wonderful if you never fell back into old ways once you achieved this state, but in truth, life throws you some tests now and then to see if you have learned the lesson and can apply it to other areas of your life.

I remember writing a final exam in university, or maybe it was in high school, I can't remember. The last question on the exam was worth a lot of marks, and when I read it, I was immediately stumped. Then I thought, I bet the teacher has written this in such a way to see if we really understand what she taught us. I kept staring at it. She must have seen the smoke coming from my head. During the exam, she walked up and down between the rows of desks, and as she passed me, she quietly said, "You know how to do this." Her words must have watered the "I know it" seed within because my thoughts switched from, *I don't know. I'm going to give up,* to *I can figure this out. I can do it.* The power of suggestion and the power one person's belief in me made all the difference as I continued to search my brain for the answer. My eyes flicked back and forth between the ticking clock and the paper. All of a sudden it came to me and excitedly I said, "I got it." I wrote at lightning speed because by this point I had less than ten minutes left. It was a math question, and I wrote all the steps in order and felt confident that I got the answer she was looking for. I remember feeling so excited because in the end, I did learn the concept and I also learned how to apply it to a different scenario. I also learned the power of belief. I can't remember what the math question was about, and even if I did, I might not remember how to solve it now, but the bigger lessons I carry with me to this day. What a great exam!

My math exam serves as a metaphor for life. Situations present themselves and instead of drawing on a new belief that serves you - *I am worthy, and I can do it!* - it is common to respond with an old belief that no longer serves you such as *I can't do this. Who are you to think you can do this?* The new beliefs aren't rooted into your subconscious, yet to a certain degree, the old ones are, so if you act without awareness and your default response contains old information (aka beliefs) you can slip back into old ways in the blink of an eye. You might be quick to criticize yourself when this happens, but there is no value in that. Would you criticize a child who is trying to learn something new or would you gently go over how to do it, cheer her on, and offer her support and encouragement? It's valuable to notice your response and then make the necessary adjustments. With practice and repetition, your new ways of thinking will take root. You will begin catching yourself before you act and eventually the responses you desire will become your new default responses. It's a process, one to notice and not judge. One that shows you where you are and what your next steps might be. You can see it as an opportunity to celebrate the changes you have made and express gratitude for how far you have come or kick yourself for falling back into old ways. I personally prefer to be loved rather than kicked. **Remember, gratitude will bring you more of what you desire. Be kind to the child within who is working hard to heal and change.**

It's important to keep in mind that as you travel through the place in between and adopt new beliefs and ways of thinking, you might find yourself questioning systems, traditions, and ways of interacting. Allow the curious mind you had as a two-year-old to come alive again. Two-year-olds constantly ask, "Why?" For a two-year-old, everything is new, and they ask why as a means of understanding the information they are being given. Allow yourself to be in this space again. When you are letting go of beliefs that no longer serve you and are looking for new ones that do, get curious. Ask yourself why you are doing the things you are doing.

Open Your Journal

- Are you doing something that you don't want to do? Describe it. Why are you doing it?

- Are you going somewhere that you don't want to go? Why?

- Where was your last holiday? What made you decide to go there?

- Why do you wear the clothes that you wear?

- Why do you eat certain foods or cook in a certain style?

- What is your parenting style? Why?

- How do you relate to your boss? Why?

- How do you talk to your partner? Why?

- Do you insist your children take music lessons, dress a certain way or act a certain way? Why?

Why, why, why? Become curious! Notice what feels right and what doesn't. Look for the "should." Notice what you do and what you go along with without question. Is it time to question it? If it doesn't feel right then, I would say yes, the time has come.

The family system is often a big area of question. Where did you get your views on how a family *should* look and operate? Did you make a conscious choice about what your family system looks like or did you create the one you have based on old beliefs and what you experienced growing up? If the beliefs serve you, that's great. Keep going. Maybe your current system looks as it does because of what you don't want. That takes some pondering! You know what you don't want so you strive to not create it, but you never really get clear on what you do want. Family systems have changed significantly over the years and if people have an old belief about how a family system *should* look, then how easy would it be to feel like you have failed if your family doesn't match this picture and expectation? What if you and your family opened up to the idea that there are many ways of being a family and explored what was right for your family? Families can take on different appearances and be highly functional. What is your belief? Does it serve you and your family and allow all members to thrive?

Your health, or ill health, can be a way your body is trying to tell you that you are living your life in a *should* mode versus an *honoring* mode? How many people are experiencing depression because they are not living true to what feels right for them? If something isn't working in your life, whether it be a relationship, your work environment or your health, look to see if *should* is a contributing factor. The next time you are irritated or edgy, notice if a *should* is at work. What would it feel like to do what you desire to do versus what you feel you *should* do? Maybe depression and irritation are your body's way of talking to you?

Here are a few more clues that a *should* is at work. Do you spend time and energy trying to fit in? Do you justify what you are doing or attempt to make sense of what you are doing? Do you talk a lot? If so, what are you saying? And, to whom? Are you attempting to convince others or yourself of your choices?

Remember, how you show up in one area of your life is how you show up in all areas so as you begin exploring the "should's," you are going to begin noticing them everywhere! It's okay. Choose to have some fun with it. You might say out loud, Oh, I'm *should-ing* on myself again!" This new way of looking at life allows you to make changes in how you show up in your workplace, your personal and business relationships and as a parent to name a few. Listen for the *should*. Listen for the justifications. Notice what feels right. Notice what doesn't. It's all great information!

Open Your Journal

- Can you think of instances where you said *"should"* or feel like you *"should"* do something? Jot those incidents down. Why do you feel you should do it?

- What do you gain by doing it? (Acceptance? Keeping the peace? Maintaining tradition?)

- What is your fear or concern about not doing it?

- What would feel right for you to do?

- Remember, what someone thinks or says tells you where they are at. What you do and how you respond tells you where you are at. Are you ready to make some changes?

- If yes, what is one step you can take?

Place 14

On Motivation

"Some people make it happen. Some people watch it happen. Some people wonder what happened."

~ Anonymous

Do you have days when you have a skip in your step and then days when you can hardly step? As I became more attuned to my feelings and my energy level, I noticed when I was purposeful and excited about something, I had incredible energy and motivation, whereas when I was unclear and uncertain, my energy level and motivation were low. I realize this is not a big revelation for many people. What I want to bring awareness to is how easy it is to veer off the path of passion, one step at a time, often without knowing it. Let's look at how that can happen. Have you ever noticed when you gain insight on something or start something new that you feel excited and your energy and motivation increase? Maybe you gained some insight on how you want to move forward in your life, or you gained some awareness around what has you stuck. Maybe a new opportunity has come your way that you said yes to and it feels great. Regardless of what put the skip into your step, it's there. Insight and clarity created a new beacon of light for you and has ignited your motivation. Getting up each day becomes easier because you have a new focus and hope. Your current life doesn't stop just because you had an ah-ha moment, which is why it is key to keep your new insights in the forefront of your mind and be intentional about weaving action steps into your day. Busy days and habitual responses can pull you away from the new course you decided to chart. Even the most aware person has fallen prey to veering off course when she fails to check in daily with her intentions, goals, and desires.

Taking steps to the right and left as you journey toward an intended goal or vision is normal, and if you are constantly checking in with your end goal, corrections can be made along the way. Failure to do so can result in falling way off course. Airplane pilots understand this concept completely. I read that airline pilots are only on course a small percentage of time during any flight. They spend most of the flight correcting their flight path because turbulence and other factors cause them to go off course. Sounds like most people's days! A GPS with a clear, specific destination programmed into it ensures they arrive at the intended destination. What would happen if they weren't using a GPS with clear particulars? How would they know they were off course? What indicators would they have? What would happen if they didn't make the subtle corrections throughout the flight? If there were no indicators, they wouldn't know to make corrections. And if there were indicators but they didn't make the necessary corrections, arriving at their intended destination would be highly unlikely.

If you are unclear about what you want your life to look and feel like, then there is nothing to key into your GPS. You have no intended destination. Author Lewis Carroll wrote, *"If you don't know where you are going, any road will take you there."* Have you ever heard yourself say, "This is not what I expected?" Ask yourself if you were clear about what you wanted. You might be clear about what you don't want and do well at avoiding it. However, if you aren't clear about what you do want, you have nothing to program into your GPS. As a result, you live a life of avoidance - avoiding what you don't want, but not getting what you do want because you haven't taken the time to identify what exactly it is that you want. You cannot put an address into a GPS if you don't know what it is. If you do know what you desire, but fail to chart your course with regular checks to see if what you are currently doing is leading you there, then you are much like a pilot who has no GPS. There will be no indications that you are off course and no opportunity for course corrections. You just keep on going, full steam ahead to anywhere or nowhere! Suffice to say, it is unlikely you will arrive at your intended destination. Below is a story of what happened to a passenger jet when the flight coordinates were off by just 2 degrees.

In 1979, a large passenger jet with 257 people on board left New Zealand for a sightseeing flight to Antarctica and back. Unknown to the pilots, someone had modified the flight coordinates by a mere 2 degrees. This error placed the aircraft 28 miles (45 km) to the east of where the pilots assumed they were. As they approached Antarctica, the pilots descended to a lower altitude to give the passengers a better look at the landscape. Although both were experienced pilots, neither had made this particular flight before, and they had no way of knowing that the incorrect coordinates had placed them directly in the path of Mount Erebus, an active volcano that rises from the frozen landscape to a height of more than 12,000 feet (3,700 meters). As the pilots flew onward, the white of the snow and ice covering the volcano blended with the white of the clouds above, making it appear as though they were flying over flat ground. By the time the instruments sounded the warning that the ground was rising fast toward them, it was too late. The airplane crashed into the side of the volcano, killing everyone on board.[3]

Do you know where you are going? How frequently do you check in to ensure you are still on course? What tools are you using as your checklist?

You too live in a dynamic and changing environment. The journey to your desires and goals will not be a straight line from point A to point B. As life happens around you, it is normal to veer to the right and to the left of your target. If you remain clear on your

3 Uchtorf, D.F (2008, April). A Matter Of A Few Degrees. Retrieved from https://www.lds.org/general-conference/2008/04/a-matter-of-a-few-degrees

destination, keep it forefront in your mind, make the necessary adjustments along the way and have checkpoints to ensure you are on the right course, the likelihood of arriving at your desired destination increases. Sometimes new opportunities come your way that feel right for you, and you consciously revisit and rewrite your goals and intended destination.

On the other hand, if you are not clear and/or do not keep your goals and intentions forefront in your mind, it is easy to veer off course. If there is never a check in point, you won't know you are off course, and eventually, you will find yourself asking the inevitable question, *How did I get here?* or maybe you hear yourself saying, *This wasn't the life I planned on having.* Did you actually have a plan? Did you check in with that plan from time to time? If years or decades have gone by before you thought to lift your head to see where you are going, you might find you are significantly off course, and it will take concerted effort and time to get back on track toward your desired goal. You might be so off track that you have no idea what you want. That's okay. It happens, and you can start today exploring and getting in touch with what you want.

Having a clear plan is one thing, and many people are learning the value of goal setting and writing down those goals. Equally important is remembering to check in with your goals and your plan to ensure you are on track. Life is dynamic. You receive new information constantly. Media, billboards, radio, conversations, and the notifications on our personal devices interrupt you continuously. The ideas and perspectives of the people in your day influence you. All of these can unintentionally lead you in a different direction. Have you ever watched how trains move from one track to another? The train is guided by the use of a mechanically installed switch. The switch consists of tapering rails, and these rails lie between the outer rails the train is currently traveling on. The tapering rails can be moved laterally in one of two directions, and they direct the train to either move onto the straight path or onto a diverging path. When a particular destination is in mind, the choice of path is intentional, and the train will be directed onto one or the other path. If the switch is not locked, the wheels of the train will force the points to move and the train will move forward based on where the wheels moved the points. In such case, the wheels, not the engineer, determined the train's direction.

Cartoons often depict this concept showing a fork in the road. In this case, however, there is the awareness of a choice. More often than not, the influences in your day cause you to function more like a train that is on a track with unlocked switches versus someone standing at a fork in the road deciding which road is best. If you are someone who is easily influenced, gets excited at new ventures and ideas, or lacks the discipline to pause before making decisions, you could be led onto a diverging path and away from your intended goals and desires. You might profess that you love change and adventure (that was me!), but in the midst of a new experience and the high that comes with it, it is easy to lose sight of a greater purpose - one that could fill your heart with a lasting high and make you feel satiated, which is different from what momentary experiences tend to offer. Pausing to consider choices can be likened to developing a muscle. With practice and repetition, the muscle becomes strong. Over time it will become habitual for you to pause before acting as well as honoring intuitive nudges. Coupled with a regular review of your goals to ensure your activities are linked to what you want, you increase the likelihood of reaching your desired destination and living the life you desire.

Physical checklists can help you stay on track and help you see what causes you to veer from your intended goals. The body also communicates such messages to you. Many do not understand the language of the body and what it is attempting to communicate, so its attempt to inform is ignored. Sometimes you even do things to silence it. Let's look at how our bodies talk to us.

Open Your Journal

I want you to ponder if you know what you want your day to look and feel like and if you feel clear about your desires or intentions. Maybe you don't know what you want, and that is okay. Remember, everything is great information. Knowing what you don't want is a great start, so don't criticize yourself if this is where you are.

- Write what comes to you when you think about what you want or don't want. I want this to be a part of your awareness as you continue on.

Remember, at the beginning of this chapter I talked about the excitement and motivation you have when you get clear about what you want and what feels right for you? When you find yourself to be less motivated than you once were, tired or easily irritated, can you see that this is the voice of the body? Many people judge their feelings and themselves. Have you ever questioned, doubted or judged yourself? Have you heard yourself ask any of the following questions?

"What's wrong with me?"

"Am I lazy?"

"Why can't I stay focused?"

"Why do I feel so overwhelmed? I should be able to handle all of this. I just need to get organized."

"I'm such a procrastinator."

Are these statements you ask or say to yourself? Is this the place you go to when you are feeling less motivated or when you have veered off path and are feeling lost? What does it feel like when you talk to yourself this way? Does it help you in any way or cause further despair? Try being kind and compassionate during such times and instead, look at your feelings of overwhelm, and lack of motivation and focus as messages from the body. Instead of criticizing yourself, become curious. The harsh statements above sound like scolding, and think about what children tend to do when scolded. Most withdraw. Some lash out and rebel. Few feel safe enough to share more of what they are feeling. The same holds true for you. When you scold your behaviors instead of understanding them, you are missing the opportunity to hear the messages your body is communicating. Gently ask yourself, *What's going on? What am I feeling? How do I feel about my current day? What's missing?*

Have you ever thought your lack of motivation is keeping you from going even further down a path that is not right for you? Give that perspective some thought. Maybe your procrastination deserves a big thank you! Please don't confuse that last statement as permission to stay stuck, rather see it as offering great information.

Open Your Journal

- Write any words or statements you have heard yourself say at times when you are feeling tired and unmotivated.

- When you are feeling unmotivated, what things are you not wanting to do? Be as specific as you can.

- Look at what you wrote, is it possible these tasks move away from your desires and what makes your heart sing?

Sometimes the people you are closest to don't offer the support you need to achieve your desires. Some even criticize your efforts. Do you realize how much energy it takes to keep their thoughts at bay?

Think about a time when you were committed to eating better, and a friend encouraged you to have "just a bite," or in my case, "just one chocolate covered almond," assuring you that one won't hurt. You know one bite usually leads to two bites and you know for sure you have never eaten just one chocolate covered almond. You also see the bigger picture and know how it's not just the one bite you are most concerned with, but rather the craving that will show up again tomorrow as a result. You have learned that none is better at this time and heading out for a walk will get your mind off the forbidden fruit and you also get some exercise and fresh air. Think about the two different trajectories that are kick started because of one small decision and how one drains your energy and the other produces energy. When people achieve the goals they desire, it is because of a hundred small decisions, not one big decision. As Lao Tzu once said, *"The journey of a thousand miles begins with one step."* Make sure the people in your life are making the steps easier not harder.

This speaks to the importance of surrounding yourself with cheerleaders. People who encourage and support you. People who remind you of your goal and who want you to succeed. People who give you strength on the days when it's hard to keep going. People who encourage you with their words and their actions.

Keep in mind that a person doesn't have to say something to drain your battery. A person's body language and lack of comment can cause a drain. If your perception of their response or lack of response is one of disapproval or judgment, it can feed your own feelings of uncertainty. Remember, until your new ways of thinking are rooted, doubt will seize every opportunity to sneak in and sabotage your success.

You can compare passive non-supportive behavior with a slow leak in your car tire. Imagine making a plan to drive across the country. You pack everything you need for the trip and program your GPS. You are set and ready to go. If unknowingly, you have a nail in your tire, or maybe drove over one along the way, and it is causing a slow leak, it is highly unlikely that you will arrive at your destination before the tire flattens and disables your car. You might stop and put gas into your car and follow the directions as indicated on your GPS, but the slow leak is working against you without your awareness. As your tire loses air, you aren't getting the mileage you did when you started out. The journey starts taking longer. The wheels begin to lose their balance because of the air loss and the ride feels bumpier than it did at the start. You question if driving across the country was a good idea. You mutter, *What was I thinking? Why did I think I could do this?* Then you tell yourself the car is fine and you are just tired of driving. You question your capability. The silent outside influence has worked its way into your mind and is sabotaging your success much like how a parasite robs the body of the nourishment it needs to thrive.

It is important to identify the people in your life who are like a slow leak in a tire and to choose wisely how much time you spend with them.

Open Your Journal

Who are the cheerleaders in your life? These people support you and encourage you. They are the ones who say, "Let's go for a walk" when they see you considering a food choice that steers you away from your goals. They breathe confidence and belief into you when you are running short on your own.

- Who are the energy drainers? Some will be quite obvious. It's the less obvious energy drainers in your life that can do the most damage. Can you identify them?

As you travel through the place in between and develop new thoughts, beliefs and habits, it takes time for your confidence to develop and become rock solid. Visualize a newly planted sapling. It is vulnerable and greatly affected by its environment. Sometimes the person who planted it will put stakes around it to offer it support. Sometimes they will put burlap around it to protect it from the winter elements. They nurture and protect it until its trunk grows thick and strong and its roots grow deep and wide. Once this happens, the tree can stand on its own and has the ability to handle the day-to-day elements it encounters. Think of yourself as that sapling. Are the people in your life acting as stakes and burlap or are they acting more like a cold wind or a heavy foot that seeks to destroy?

When you set out to achieve a desired goal, it takes time for your confidence and belief to develop to the level needed to be unaffected by the elements around you. Seldom is it rock solid at the onset, so if you are doing something outside your comfort zone or if you are choosing to walk on a path that is different than the path others are walking on, the influences around you, even a disapproving look, can have a significant impact. **Set yourself up for success. Choose to share your goals with people who support you. Spend time with people who encourage you, nourish you and believe in you.**

I just talked at length about how people can affect your motivation. Now let's look at another possibility. Is it possible that your current goal no longer feels right to you? Maybe it needs to be tweaked in some way. Or maybe a complete makeover is required. Years ago, I met someone who shared with me that he became a dentist because it was what his dad wanted. Years later, he finally gave himself permission to do what he wanted. How hard would it be to stay motivated when you aren't doing what makes your heart sing? Are you doing what you want to be doing or what someone else wants you to do? Sometimes you make a choice thinking it is going to look and feel a certain way, but it is completely different from your expectations. Do you recognize that and give yourself permission to make some changes? As you travel towards any goal, life brings forth new experiences, information, and awareness. There are many reasons you are where you are and your experiences all have value. Sometimes a little tweak is all that is needed for your motivation and passion to resume. Sometimes, a bigger change is required.

Avoid judging and criticizing your decisions. Instead, see where you are as offering great information and providing valuable pieces of the puzzle. Pursue your curiosity.

Open Your Journal

Have a dialogue with yourself by asking the following questions:

- I had a lot of energy, and now it is gone. I am not a lazy person, so what is this all about?

- What am I feeling?

- Maybe I don't want to do (fill in the blank) because it's no longer a fit for me. Is that possible?

- What or who is draining my battery?

- Are there any moments in my day when I feel motivated and have high energy? What am I doing?

- When am I least motivated?

Become curious. It's okay for something to have felt right at one point in your life and now it no longer feels right for you. When you show compassion and kindness to yourself and become a trusted friend to your inner self, the answers will come. Your intuition will speak freely, and when it does, it allows you to see why and how you veered from your path. Sometimes the information comes quickly. Sometimes you simply need to allow time for the answers to come. Giving it permission to come and opening up to it is the place to start. Often, I will say, *Send me a sign. I am open to seeing it in whatever form it comes.* My request is always answered.

Here are a few examples of how this took place in my life. Remember, messages seldom come in an envelope in the mail with your name neatly written on it and a subject line that reads: "Your answer to XYZ!" (though I did get a piece of mail one time that offered a solution!).

A while back, I noticed my motivation level was low with regard to work. I asked the Universe to send a message and help me understand what was going on for me. Soon after, I felt compelled to call the coach I was working with and acted on my impulse. I didn't have a scheduled appointment, and I wasn't really sure what I was going to say to him. The fact that I didn't have an appointment scheduled could have been reason enough to talk myself out of making the call. Before any doubt set in, I dialed his number. I was surprised that he answered and I said sheepishly, "Hi, I don't really know why I am calling."

He graciously gave me some time, and we explored the question I had for him, but at the end of our call, I didn't feel much clearer than I did at the beginning of the call. I didn't judge my decision to call him. I agreed to continue acting on any intuitive nudges trusting each was a stepping stone and leading me to the information I desired. I also became curious. Over the next couple of days, I noticed the words, "all in" come to me in different ways. When I was speaking with my coach, the word "all" came up for different reasons. Although I was open to messages in whatever form they came, I thought there must be a message contained in these words. Why else would they keep showing up and why would I be noticing them? I googled, "all in." I saw that it was the title of a book by Arlene Dickinson so off to the library I went and signed out the book. Sure enough, more pieces came. Do you see where I am going with my story? I felt like I was on a treasure hunt! Since I remembered treasure hunts being fun, I decided to see the process as fun. In the end, guess what happened? I gained understanding about why my motivation level dropped and what I needed to do to get back on track. Remember, I didn't even know I was off track. What I knew was that I was unmotivated, and I began judging and criticizing myself and even began wondering if I was simply being lazy.

When you are stuck, unmotivated, or lacking the desired skip in your step, ask the Universe for a message and open up to the different ways it might come to you. Look at the sequences in your life and become curious. What messages are they attempting to deliver? Go on a treasure hunt. Put your Sherlock Holmes hat on and see where you are led and what is revealed to you. Give yourself permission to have some fun discovering what has affected your motivation.

Be open to the different ways the messages come to you. Be willing to hear and understand what is presenting. I have yet to find that letter in my mailbox with neat writing saying, "This envelope contains the answers to the question you asked on Monday." **When you are open, receptive and patient, the messages you need will surely come. Stay with the process.** Sometimes you will feel like you are on a treasure hunt. Choose to embrace the process and have fun with it.

Place 15

Our Relationship With Money

"If someone asked you for $5.00, and you only had $1.00 in your pocket, can you help them?"
~ Rita Davenport

The topic of money is both huge and significant, which is why there are shelves upon shelves on the topic in libraries and bookstores. At some point, as you travel through the place in between, the need to explore your relationship with money will appear because it is linked to feeling worthy. What is your belief about money? What is your relationship with money? Are you active in your financial planning? Is talking about money comfortable or uncomfortable? Does your spouse handle all of the finances? Do you handle all of the finances? Do you have more month than money at the end of every month?

Your beliefs and relationship with money are as important to your health and well-being as food and exercise. Are you someone who knows very little about money and gets squeamish at the thought of talking about it? Maybe you ignore it hoping everything works out. How do your beliefs about money affect your behaviors? If the place in between is about change and moving from one space to another, a good question to ask is, "How do my current beliefs and understanding of money affect my ability to make the changes I desire?"

Open Your Journal

- Close your eyes and think back to when you were a young child. Think about an experience that involved money. Describe the experience and how you interpreted it. Maybe you asked for something, wanted something, or broke something. What comes to mind? Write about your experience and how you felt.

- Did you hear your parents talk about money or make references to money? Did you ever hear the saying, *"Money doesn't grow on trees?"* What else did you hear regarding money? Jot down what comes to you.

Our experiences leave imprints and beliefs are created from these imprints. What beliefs about money did you create from the experiences you had? Are these beliefs helping you live the life you desire or holding you back from doing so?

It is essential to become aware of the beliefs we have about money, how they affect our life and our ability or inability to embrace the changes we desire. I encourage you to make a concerted effort to learn about money and your relationship with it. See the reference section at the back of this book for recommendations. Taking responsibility for your financial health is a key component in living the life you desire.

Let me offer some examples on how beliefs we hold about money not only affect various areas of our life, but also our choices and aspirations. Circle any statement you recall hearing or that you currently feel is true:

- Working long, hard hours is the way to generate an income.

- You have to work hard to get what you want in life.

- Being an employee with a good company brings security.

- I'm grateful to have a good job.

- My value is linked to how much I produce or do each day.

I picked up many beliefs along the way, and without knowing it, they led to feelings of being worthy or not worthy. What do you feel worthy of? What do you feel unworthy of? If amounts of worthiness were put into boxes like age ranges are on questionnaires, what box would you be checking? With age, there is the opportunity to get into the next box. Is there a cap on your worthiness based on your beliefs? How do those feelings and beliefs affect how you show up in the world?

When did worthiness get linked to dollars and what a person can have both financially and emotionally? When and how did that happen? I work with a lot of women and feeling worthy is a common issue I see. My curious mind wonders why so many women feel unworthy (I was on that list a few years ago and haven't gotten completely off it yet, although I am making progress). Could it be linked to messages we heard about money when we were young, which turned into a belief and led to us leading a life based on that belief? What beliefs about money are currently running your life?

Let's look at how the beliefs above can keep you stuck when deep within, you desire to do something different. What if you hold a belief that being an employee is the only way to ensure financial security and now you have a strong yearning to step away from your current work and become an entrepreneur? What if you believe you don't have what it takes to be an entrepreneur? What if you have a lucrative career but it doesn't make your heart sing, and you want to leave it to pursue passions that are coming from deep within? What if you no longer want to work the traditional work week that you have been conditioned to believe is normal and brings security? Do your current beliefs about money support what you feel is right to do or do they hold you back from taking action? If any of these questions are causing you to raise an eyebrow or flinch a bit, exploring your relationship with money will have great value for you.

Have you ever been asked, "If money wasn't a factor, what would you do?" I remember being asked that question on several occasions. I also remember struggling with my answer. Reflecting back, I can see how my imagination shrunk to match the beliefs I held about what was possible for me. Since what I truly desired fell outside of the beliefs I had about money, and what I could achieve, my options list didn't make my heart sing, but it did match my current beliefs about how much money I could generate and what I could do. I'm sure you have noticed when you ask a child what she wants to do when she grows up, she quickly speaks what comes to her. She doesn't check her bank account first to see if she can afford her desires. She doesn't think being an actress or an astronaut is out of this world!

When did you shift from thinking you could do anything to narrowing your thinking and shrinking your options list? What came off of the list? This awareness is so important because you might spend your whole life seeking achievements that fit into the worthy box you put yourself in versus a life that makes your heart sing. The desires that lit the fires within you when you were young never die. They might become dimmed, but they constantly tug at you, and I believe it is this tug from deep within that creates the discontentment you feel, along with the desire for more. Let go of the guilt around this feeling. Let go trying to override the feeling with words convincing you that you *should* be happy with the life you have.

You can't override the tug. I believe all of us were put on this earth for a special reason and there will be no rest deep within until we meet that end. There might be lots of side stepping, justifying, excuses, and attempts to convince yourself that you should be grateful for what you have. It has nothing to do with not being grateful. It has everything to do with not living true to you and your life's purpose. Don't confuse the two, and know that you, and everyone on this planet, is worthy and deserving of living in a way that feels right and ignites the fires within. If you have been determined to figure out what is holding you back, good for you. Personal growth is some of the hardest, yet most rewarding work that you will ever do.

Open Your Journal

- Can you recall a dream or a desire you had as a kid, a teen, or as an adult? Describe it.

- When did it get put on the back shelf or taken off of the options list and why?

- Did the messages you heard about how to make money or how you are to show up in life have anything to do with your desires being put aside?

Your view on money can serve as a mirror. Mirrors reflect what is in front of them. How you view money reflects how you view yourself. Do you fear it? Does it control you? Do you attempt to control it? How you handle money or treat money can mirror how you treat yourself, or allow yourself to be treated. Sit with that thought for a few minutes.

I remember a time when I used to say that having physical things didn't make a person happy and I believed spiritual and emotional richness was the path to happiness. I have since learned that happiness isn't something to be compartmentalized and optimal well-being requires all aspects to be developed and embraced. Is a hand better than a foot? Would you want to give up one to have the other? Additionally, I learned that even when you choose to live simply, you need money.

I learned what I was really doing at that time was justifying my lack of money, and my thoughts and way of living were in accord with the beliefs I had about money. I had enough to make ends meet, but seldom was there money left for the pleasures in life. This was a common pattern in my adult life. It became apparent while traveling through the place in between that it was time to explore my beliefs and patterns if I wanted a different outcome from what I experienced in the past.

Instead of seeing that I was capable and worthy of making more money, I created a belief that I didn't need it. My lifestyle reflected my beliefs about money. My spending discretions and decisions mirrored what I learned as I was growing up. During these years, I was unable to see money as an energy nor could I see my acceptance or resistance of it linked to what I witnessed and learned while I was growing up. Neither was truth per se, simply beliefs that were at the helm of my potential and purpose. Eventually, I learned that for my potential and purpose to be realized, I needed new understanding and new beliefs at the helm.

How many times have you heard a "rags to riches" story? *Forbes Magazine* has featured articles on millionaires and billionaires who didn't attend college or dropped out. In addition to confidence and drive, beliefs about money were always at the root of these success stories. Let's look at another scenario: lottery winners. Statistics indicate that a high percentage of lottery winners eventually find themselves either broke or in the same financial situation they were in before they won the lottery. Regardless of how large the winnings, if the winners did not change their beliefs around money and their worthiness, they squandered it away until they were back to a state that aligned with their beliefs.

There are many people who have risen above adversity or moved from one economic demographic to a higher one. Such individuals consciously shifted their mindset and embraced beliefs to support their goals. They were committed and willing to break patterns of behavior that did not serve them. Some of these individuals had great cheerleaders. Some had a few cheerleaders, but moreover, they had an internal conviction and a determination to live differently.

Money is an energy, and while it is called a currency, look at the word within currency: current. Consider looking at money as a current. Are you flowing with it and open to its abundance or are you resisting it, feeling unworthy of it, attempting to control it or fearing it? Beliefs around money will need to be explored as you travel through the place in between. You live in a physical world that uses money to buy the things you need. That isn't likely to change anytime soon. What can change is your beliefs around how it is generated, how much you have and the amounts you feel worthy of having. How would life be different for you if you let go of any beliefs about money that no longer serve you and embraced new beliefs that empower you and allow you to step into the flow of abundance? What would happen if instead of focusing on making money, you tapped into your own worth first? How would that change the flow of money coming to you? Are you ready to feel worthy? Are you ready to look within first?

Your beliefs affect your thoughts, which then affect your feelings and in turn your actions. **If you explore your beliefs around money and open up to the possibility of living authentically, is it possible that the energy around money would change and it would flow more easily and abundantly to you? Would it allow you to step into your true power and money would just be a natural by-product? What if it is not about working harder to achieve more money, but rather stepping into your worthiness as a means of tapping into its flow?**

Open Your Journal

- On a scale of 1-10, 1 being low and 10 being high, what number best describes how worthy you feel of living the life you desire?

- Close your eyes and let go of your current belief around your worthiness. Connect with the deepest part of yourself and see a flowing river. See yourself in that flow feeling free and joyous. See abundance around you. See the leaves on a tree and the blades of grass that could never be counted. Notice the air that is always there and ready for you to take in. Feel the abundance and fullness that nature offers. You are a part of that abundance and flow. Sit in this space. Feel it as fully as you can. See and feel yourself being worthy of endless abundance. How does that feel?

- How would your life be different if you could live from this place?

What if this was the definition of money: "*A medium for exchange that is acquired by tapping into your creativity and your unique gifts and putting them into the world. It is an infinite source that lies within each person.*" Everyone has gifts to bring to this world, and everyone's gifts are highly valuable and needed. It is humans who assigned a value on them and deemed their worthiness in monetary terms. Are you ready to let go of any beliefs and stories about money that no longer serve you?

Your beliefs around money will either propel you forward or hold you back, have you feeling excited and purposeful, or fear-filled. If you are stuck in any area of your life, have a look to see if there is a belief about money at the root. As I said earlier in the chapter, exploring your relationship with money is a study unto itself and may be one of the greatest studies you will partake in, for I am seeing how it links to every area of our life. Louise Hay has always been at the core of my learning. Her books, *Empowering Women, You Can*

Heal Your Life, and her co-authored book with Cheryl Richardson, *You Can Create An Exceptional Life* all contain chapters on money. Other authors from whom I have gained insight and awareness include, *Think and Grow Rich for Women* by Sharon Lechter, *All In* by Arlene Dickinson, *Women and Money* by Suze Orman, *Money - A Love Story* by Kate Northrup and *Beautiful Money* by Leanne Jacobs.

We live in a physical world that requires money. Money brings choice and empowerment, and it is the current form of currency we use as a means of exchange. The amount of money we allow to flow into our life is based on our current beliefs. Everyone needs money to live and the more money we allow in, the more we can put back into the world. Be a part of the river and at the same time feed the river. Rita Davenport, former President of Arbonne International and author of *Funny Side Up* says, *"Money is not everything, but it is right up there with oxygen."*

Remember, money is both an inside and an outside job. The exercise earlier in this chapter helped you identify your current beliefs about money. Write down an action step you are going to take to explore and change beliefs that no longer serve you. Perhaps you will read some of the books I recommended. Maybe you will hire a coach to help you change current limiting beliefs. **Decide on one action step and commit to taking it. Remember, without action, nothing changes.**

To live your highest life, to have a desirable relationship with yourself and others, and to achieve personal goals and career desires, it is essential that you explore your relationship with money and the power that lies deep within. If you find yourself stuck in any area of your life, looking through these windows will bring valuable insight to what has you stuck and why.

Place 16

Prepare For Shifts In Your Relationships

"You have to let go of what was to welcome what will be."
~ Cheryl Richardson

You might notice that when one thing changes in your life, it can start an avalanche of change in all other areas of your life. Why is that? How you show up in one area of your life is how you show up in all areas of your life and without your awareness, your interactions with the different people become comfortable and familiar, and over time, patterns develop. Are you a decision maker, someone who needs to be right, or a peacekeeper? Depending on your tendencies, you will attract people who can balance the interaction. For example, if you love making decisions, it is likely that you will be drawn to people who are okay if you make the decision. Can you see how this relationship would feel comfortable and create a harmonious interaction?

Think about what happens when you meet someone who also feels the need to make the final decision all the time. What tends to happen in this situation? Chances are neither of you do much to foster the relationship because both of you want to occupy the same role. In this situation, for the relationship to be enjoyable, one or both of you would have to be okay with not having the final say constantly. There is some truth in the saying, "opposites attract" and understanding why opposites tend to attract is important. Often, the relationship you have with someone is less about whether they are opposite from you, but rather do they allow you to live according to the beliefs and ways of interacting that you know? Another way of saying that is, do they keep the story you are telling yourself alive and true?

The above example illustrates how you attract people into your life based on what is comfortable and familiar which tends to mirror what you experienced growing up, the roles you held in your family, and the beliefs you currently hold. There are other factors linked to the relationships you create. One is how you perceive yourself and your level of self-esteem. If you have a strong sense of self and high self-esteem, it is unlikely that you will find yourself in the company of people who belittle you, knock you down, are negative or try to hold you back in any way. That said, you can have high esteem in some areas of your life and low esteem in other areas of your life. The company you keep will reflect this.

Have a look at the relationships you are currently in. As you move through the place in between and get to know yourself better, are you noticing aspects of your relationships that no longer feel okay? Can you see the learning opportunity your partner, co-worker, friend or all of the above are bringing to you? If you look closely, you will see similarities within different relationships, so it makes sense that when one relationship reaches a point where you are motivated to make changes, eventually these changes are brought into the other relationships too.

Open Your Journal

- What relationships in your life no longer feel right or bring you joy?

- Can you identify what doesn't feel right? If so, write about it.

When you make a change in one area of your life, there is a ripple effect, and all areas of your life tend to be affected. Did you think your partner was different than your father or mother, only to see years later that he or she is more alike than different from one or both of your parents? The person might possess qualities that are different, and perhaps this is in part what drew you to him or her, but often there are qualities and roles that each of you hold that create a sense of comfort and familiarity. The same can hold true with a friend or your employer. It can also present with a sibling or a child. This is when life can really turn up the volume! Family and friends can definitely be your greatest teachers. You will feel less agitated and more empowered when you see that the world around you is not changing, it is you who is changing. You are simply seeing what has been there all along and sometimes what has been there all along is binding and limiting. At the very least, you will begin to make sense of some of the interactions you are having as well as the feelings you may have been struggling with, sometimes for years.

There are different kinds of people and relationships in your life. Some seem to shine light on lessons you need to learn and wounds you need to heal. There may be people in your life who are also in the place in between, and they are seeing patterns in their relationships, including the relationship they have with you. These patterns may be comfortable and familiar, but not necessarily ideal, and they too are open and willing to explore the patterns with you. Together, the two of you create a safe place for each other to make important changes with awareness and compassion.

Are there people in your life that you aspire to be like? What does it feel like for you when you think about being more like them or having the life they have? What messages do you hear in your head? Can you hear the reason why you can't do or be that which you desire? Whose voice are you really hearing?

Then there are the people in your life who are casting the light for you to step into. These are people who see your greatness. They see the goodness in you, and they are offering encouragement, courage, and love to you with the pure intent of helping you find it within yourself. These people are a blessing in your life, and they often offer clean and unbiased support because they have done a lot of their own personal work. As you develop compassion for yourself and criticize yourself less, you will begin to notice you offer those same kindnesses to others. You can only offer to others what you give to yourself and have within. Do you have such a person in your life? Can you accept this person's support and love? **Can you tell the difference between people who are trying to hold you back and people who are encouraging and supportive, and honor your desires, whatever they may be?**

As you heal, grow, rebuild, and become stronger, it will lead to loving and honoring yourself and feeling worthy of all you desire. During the process, you can expect the roles you play to change. As you move along this path, needing the approval of others will lessen because the only approval you will need is that which comes from deep within yourself. There is no need to feel guilty. There is no need to continue playing a role that no longer serves you. You can make gentle changes and acknowledge what you are willing to do and not willing to do. This isn't meant to offend but to honor both you and others. There is great value in stepping into a new role that serves you, one that gives both you and others the permission to do what feels right. Someone shed light on this possibility for me, and now I desire to do the same. What a nice thing to pay forward: permission to be you and do what feels right for you.

Open Your Journal

- Look at some of the major relationships in your life. What do you like about them? What do you dislike about them?

- How does the relationship support your current way of thinking or a role you like to fill?

- Does the relationship elevate and encourage you or does it serve to keep the story you are telling yourself (which usually has limitations) true?

Pondering these questions before entering each relationship would be exhausting and maybe even paralyzing. This book calls us to connect with our feelings, lean into them, and do what feels right, instead of over analyzing them. Here is where it gets tricky. Does it feel right because it is familiar and comfortable? Or does it feel right because it supports what you desire? You might be thinking, *Good grief! How does one know the difference?* Good question.

I remember my first year in university. I did not attend university right after high school. Instead I took a long break and returned a decade later as a mature student. This meant I was a decade older than most of my peers. The first day of each class was filled with anticipation. Who would be in the class? Would I stand out like a sore thumb? What was it going to be like? I walked into each class and would quickly scan the room looking for clues to where I should sit. Where would I feel the most comfortable? Upon walking into one of the classrooms, the decision was easy. At the very back of the classroom, I spotted another mature student, as we were referred to, who was staring at me and smiling. There was an empty seat beside her, and I made a beeline for it. We wasted no time introducing ourselves, and there was giddiness around feeling like we weren't alone in this new environment littered with young, innocent faces. The wise professor started the year by bringing our desire for comfort to our attention. He commented on how it is our natural tendency to sit beside someone who appears to be like us. In my case, I was looking to match age. Others might sit beside someone who dresses the same, has a tattoo or who displays a certain attitude. He went on to say that we have the most to learn from the people who are different from us, not just different in appearance but also different in personality and behaviors. He said our tendency in new situations is to seek what feels familiar. Interesting thought.

Let's go back to opposites attracting. In such cases, is it possible the attraction occurs because an individual possesses a trait or way of behaving that you desire to have? Sometimes, you are drawn to someone because there is a feeling of familiarity and comfort. Other times you are attracted to someone because they are different from you and possess the qualities you desire to have. To add a bit more confusion to the pot, sometimes opposites attract to maintain familiar patterns of interaction and to keep the story you are telling yourself true. This is done at an unconscious level. How do you know which one is at play? Your intuition knows the answer, but what if you silenced your intuition and the wise voice within and replaced it with "should" and expectations? It's never too late to awaken your intuition. Another way of saying this is, begin consulting your body versus your head for the answers and guidance you seek. Your body is wise. Notice where you get feelings and sensations in your body. Begin to learn its language.

Given the above information, is it possible to begin looking at your interactions with more curiosity? Have you ever heard the phrase, *"When the student is ready, the teacher appears?"* You learn the most when in relationship with others. Your relationships can serve many different purposes and can bring comfort for different reasons. I have a friend who I met in Grade 5, and I love my time with her. We see and hear each other without judgment and I always feel her support and encouragement. My heart is filled to overflowing when we are together. This is a healthy and treasured relationship. There are relationships that feel good but for a different reason. These relationships might be centered around keeping you stuck and not reaching for your potential. They give you permission to play small. In fact, they encourage you to play small, and they keep your current story about yourself and your life true. In truth, these relationships don't feel good at all, but they are familiar, and sometimes, familiar feels good even when it's bad.

Relationships can teach valuable life lessons, and they can create the opportunity to practice what you are learning. Some people will cheer you on, and some people will teach you the value in learning to say no. There are infinite reasons why people come in and out of our lives. Jim Rohn says, *"You become the average of the 5 people you spend the most time with."* I mentioned this in a previous chapter, and it is worth noting again. **Who you spend your time with is a choice, and it reflects what is going on inside of you.** What is going on inside? What is your gut feeling? Let it lead you.

Now, I find it interesting to notice who I am drawn to, who I feel intimidated by, and who I sense as dangerous (emotionally and mentally, more than physically). At the forefront of my mind, I remember who I want to become, and what my dreams and goals are. With that in mind, I carefully consider who I spend my time with, and mindfully allow people and experiences into my life that support, encourage and teach me.

As you travel through the place in between and along the "discover me" continuum, you will gain increased clarity about who you are, what you desire, and how you want your life to look and feel like. You will see how learned beliefs and values created the life you have now, how they create a sense of belonging for you, and how you make choices that reflect those beliefs and the need to belong. If beliefs are at the base of your decision-making process, then it makes sense for your various relationships to have common patterns, and why when you begin to shift your perspective and create new beliefs, all areas of your life are likely to be affected to some degree.

Sometimes, you grow with people, while other times you out-grow them. What we know for sure is that change is constant, so if you are someone who resists change or feels guilty for wanting to change, ask yourself why. It is a normal and necessary part of life.

Years ago, a minister I had tremendous respect for gave the following response when I was criticized for changing. He said, "You have changed jobs, cities, are married now, and have a child. I sure hope you have changed." Enough said. Change is normal and essential. Let go of the fear around it. Read on if that doesn't sound so easy.

I read that men enter into marriage hoping their wife stays the same, and women enter marriage hoping their husband changes. If this is the case, it helps understand the high divorce rate. In his book, *Who Moved My Cheese?* Spencer Johnson states that change causes people to feel fear and anxiety because they lack the tools and the language they need to deal with change. Accepting and managing change is an important life skill, yet few people learn anything about it. If we are not taught about change, it makes sense that people fear it and seek to control it. When you make decisions based on fear, the decision may not be what is right for you but rather what you want to avoid. It is said that people are more likely to take action when it moves them away from pain than when it moves them toward pleasure. Given that many people don't feel worthy, it sure explains a lot of decisions. It also can help explain why some relationships (personal and business) end with hard feelings versus support and well wishes. If people don't feel worthy, change can be difficult, and for people in your world who also suffer from a low sense of worthiness, it can be difficult for them to support you as you step into new and more honoring ways.

It is normal to begin taking on certain roles in your relationships. Often, the roles you take on are based on what you witnessed growing up. If this is the case, then they are taken on without thought and awareness. As you get in touch with your desires and parts of yourself that you have denied, it may no longer feel right to take on a particular role. For example, until you to learn to love yourself, you might find that you tend to give, but not receive. Perhaps your days are spent filling everyone's cup but yours.

Now, you are noticing that you feel some resentment creeping in as you give to others and start criticizing yourself for having such feelings. Your journey to the self is leading you to feel worthier and is awakening the part of you who is ready to see how you constantly give and never receive. You are ready to shift this pattern. No longer do you want to fill the role of giver only, and you begin doing things differently. You might say no to a request, or maybe you start doing more things to nurture yourself. The response from the people in your relationships might vary and range from complete support and encouragement to comments attempting to degrade you and prevent you from feeling worthy so that you remain the keeper of the role they know and like. Even if it no longer serves you or your relationship, the person you are in relationship with may not be ready or willing to make the necessary changes needed for you to receive as well as give. When people in your life don't want you to change, it's more about them than it is about you. They are feeling fear and a loss of predictability and control. The change process can be everything from very rocky to smooth. It is affected by your ability to articulate and take responsibility for your feelings and the changes you want and the other person's openness to change and his/her willingness to look within. Smooth transitions take two willing people.

This can happen in all kinds of relationships. I recently saw it at play with my thirteen-year-old daughter. For eight years our New Year's Eve looked much the same: quiet night, me doing what worked for her. This past New Year's Eve, the pattern was the same. However, I noticed how disgruntled I was feeling by the end of the night. My feelings were taken up a notch because she was very inflexible and wanted the entire evening to go her way. It was easy for me to feel frustrated at her, but who taught her the pattern? It took a long walk on New Year's Day for me to see my role and to own it as well as own my desire for change. Let me just say that owning versus blaming gets a conversation about change off to a much better start!

For many people, change can be a challenging process. Living in any amount of negativity is detrimental and can sabotage your progress. If you have negativity in even one area of your life, it can wear you down and affect how you show up in the other areas of your life. If the bulk of your day is filled with negativity, the effects are compounded. To keep your will intact and your sense of worthiness strong, I encourage you to minimize the time you spend with negative, non-supportive people and to plug into outside sources that can help offset the strong influence of negativity. While you might not be able to immediately change the people with whom you spend your day, you can add positive influences to help keep you strong, focused and feeling worthy and loved. In other words, it is essential that you keep your cup filled. The most important time of day is morning. There is significant research showing the correlation between how your day starts and how your day flows. Think back to a time when your alarm didn't go off, and you slept in. Then you tripped over your slippers on the way to the bathroom. You grumbled and stated that it was going to be a lousy day. Do you remember how that day went? My guess is lousy. Studies show the pattern will continue on. Be mindful to start your day on a positive note. Before I get out of bed, I think, and often say out loud, words of gratitude. I say things like, "Thank you for a new day, thank you for a great sleep. Thank you for my health." Louise Hay taught me to thank my bed and I thank it all the time. Gratitude can be very simple and is very powerful.

There are so many things you have control over in your life and by embracing them, you will make steady change in the direction you desire. You have control over what time you get up in the morning. You have control over what you feed your brain first thing in the morning. What do you read or listen to first thing in the morning? You have control over how much water you drink, the foods you eat and how much sleep you get (it might require saying no). You have control over how you talk to yourself when you are tired. What you say when you sleep in or trip on the way to the bathroom. During the early days of the place in between, I chose to get up at 4am. I had to start work early, and I saw the value in reading first thing in the morning because I saw how it was changing my days. I learned how I started my day had a direct correlation to the kind of day I experienced. I saw the value of having a steady drip of supportive messages throughout my day. They kept my cup filled and helped to dilute any negativity I encountered. I was mindful of what I listened to in the car. I learned to tune out the negativity around me and tune into the positive, encouraging words of leaders teaching personal growth and transformation. My days began changing and over time, so did my life! I was so grateful! I wanted it to change, and when you think about it, the changes I made didn't cost a penny. It required discipline and time but no money. How many people think they need money for their lives to change? Change how you go through your day and the money will eventually come too.

Our mind is the most powerful tool in our toolkit for life. It costs nothing but costs us plenty if we don't use it wisely. I encourage you to carry recordings of mentors and people you aspire to be like on your personal devices and plug in whenever you can. Ten minutes here and there throughout your day will have a significant effect and an accumulation effect. Listen to audiobooks and podcasts in your car instead of the radio. Read even one paragraph of something before you fall asleep at night. What you take into your sleep is so important. What do you listen to, watch or read before you turn the lights out? Your beliefs about yourself will shift. Your beliefs about your future will shift and with each positive, supportive message the roots grow deeper in your psyche. Read. Listen. Plug in. What you feed your mind makes a huge difference.

As you feed your soul steady nourishment, your sense of self will strengthen. You will notice that while you are willing to be with the people in your life, you are unwilling to listen to any negative talk, especially if it is aimed at holding you back. Maybe the "old you" was a great listener, and people loved talking to you because you validated their feelings and let them stay stuck (aka a victim). There is nothing wrong with acknowledging feelings. What doesn't serve anyone is to continue talking about the same thing over and over with the belief that you have no choice. Talking about a situation in your life that you don't like simply keeps the situation alive and keeps you wallowing in it versus looking outside of it and taking responsibility for what you desire to have. You can choose to be a victim of your circumstances, but there is no value in this choice for either party. It is negative and breeds more negativity. It strengthens your belief in doom and gloom versus allowing you to see that you have choice in your life and with choice comes empowerment and with empowerment comes the opportunity to live the life you desire.

Open Your Journal

- What new habits are you committed to developing to feed and nourish your mind? Set yourself up for success by making a choice that is doable for you. For example, if morning is not your favorite time of day, start with setting your alarm 5 or 10 minutes earlier. Write an affirmation on your bathroom mirror and begin your day saying it out loud. Or, begin with changing what you listen to in your car. Small changes lead to more changes and over time create significant results. Pick one and commit to doing it.

- Who brings negativity into your life? You can mindfully and respectfully spend less time with this person. Shortening your time with someone by even 10 minutes is a step in the right direction. Recognize the value in baby steps versus all or nothing actions.

Remember to tune into the messages of the body. If you are feeling energized and in good spirits, you are on the right path. I have noticed my body speaks to me through anger, irritation, and impatience. I have been criticized on more than one occasion for having these feelings. Now I see them as trusted friends and heed their warning. Before welcoming these feelings into my life, I tried to push them down or manage them. This only led to an outburst or the feelings coming out sideways as people have heard me say. When this happens, it can cause damage, sometimes irreparable damage. At the very least, it does nothing to move me forward or create positive feelings within.

Now when I sense any of these feelings surfacing, I know they are bringing a message. When this happens, I usually find that I am in situations that are not good for me. With this awareness, I can make choices. I have come to love and appreciate my anger, irritation, and impatience. Now that I embrace them and allow their message to surface, I move forward with assertiveness and clarity versus defensiveness and fear. Outbursts have turned into calm and respect-filled conversations. My spirit is honored, and I am also able to honor the other person's spirit. The outcome is what it needs to be. It feels right to close with Louise Hay's beautiful words, *"All is well."*

Place 17

Bring On The Holidays

"When the feeling of void leaves, and there is just a space, my heart
is not empty, but full."
~ Paula Anstett

The holidays are an interesting time when you are in the place in between. I find whatever I am feeling throughout the year is heightened during the holidays. It can be compared to listening to a song on the radio you don't like, and someone turns up the volume. You become more irritated and agitated. If you have feelings of sadness within that you keep denying and pushing down, those feelings might be harder to suppress and actually heighten. Take the time to notice how you have managed these feelings in the past and if you are reading this book, it is likely you are ready to look at your feelings and take some steps toward honoring them. Hopefully, you are ready to change the goal from "Let's just get through this" to "Let's figure out what I need to do so it feels right for me."

There are so many expectations and traditions, at Christmas in particular, and they are deeply rooted regardless if they make sense or work for you anymore. If you have been doing the journal exercises, you are beginning to connect with a deeper part of yourself. You are identifying what feels right and what doesn't. You are gaining awareness and insights. You are seeing how your current beliefs have led you to where you find yourself today. Your intuition and inner knowing are waking up, and you are beginning to see in a way you have never seen before. Therefore, whatever emotions you are processing, losses you have experienced, and patterns you desire to break are likely to be heightened during this time. Consider welcoming the holidays because they will turn up the volume, they will shine an extra bright light on what feels right and what doesn't.

If you look at the thoughts and feelings you have during Christmas, and during other holidays, often they are similar to thoughts and feelings you have throughout the year. During the year, they vibrate at a lower level so you can bury them, ignore them or numb them. Holidays come with added traditions and expectations turning up the vibration. As you become more aware, you see and feel the disconnects more clearly, and they become harder to bury, ignore or numb. This is good. You don't want to "get through a holiday," instead you want to have an experience that feels right.

Holidays create a wonderful opportunity for you to simply "notice." Notice what feels right. Notice what doesn't. Notice how often you hear yourself, and others say "should." Notice how many traditions and "to-do's" are done without thought, without determining if they really fill your heart with joy. What if you had amnesia and couldn't remember past Christmases? What would you do? If you can step outside of the frenzy, you can use it as an insightful learning experience to find out what you like, what feels right and the motivation behind your actions.

Open Your Journal

- Close your eyes and picture a recent holiday in as much detail as possible. What felt right?

- What didn't feel right?

- What would you change if you could?

- What is one step you can take to make that change next time?

Easter just passed, and it led to the writing of this chapter. My family gathered on Good Friday, so Easter Sunday was a free day for me. I grew up in a Catholic family, and I remember feeling as though Easter was bigger than Christmas in our house. On Easter morning, our house was alive with colorful candy, some in plain view, some we had to search for. There was joy and excitement. We prepared for church, my sisters and I having new dresses, gloves, and hats. My brother wore a white shirt and tie. As we got older, the hats and gloves went by the wayside, but we still wore special dresses. As a family of six, we piled into our car and off to church we went to celebrate the rising of Jesus Christ.

When I moved out of my parents home, I continued many of the traditions I learned growing up. When my mom came over, I noticed she could easily find things in my kitchen because I organized my kitchen the way she did; not only was I bringing forth traditions, I was bringing forth many things I learned along the way. There is an advantage to this as long as what you are doing continues to serve you. On Sundays, I went to church because I always did. There was a piece of the tradition that brought comfort and for the most part a positive memory. As the years passed, I realized it was the quiet time I valued each Sunday morning sitting in church more than the message I was hearing. This awareness caused my ears to perk up a bit more each Sunday and take note of what I was allowing into my psyche each week as I sat with my voice silenced. I noticed I liked feeling as though I belonged, which made sense given it is a basic need of humans. This feeling came from seeing the same people week after week and exchanging greetings, but I started to see that it was rather superficial because our relationship never extended beyond a greeting or the church walls. At the end of the hour, we all went our own way, rushing to get out of the parking lot. If we truly loved being there would there be such a rush? What did I belong to?

I continued "noticing" and each week I decided what words to hold onto and which ones to let go when they didn't resonate with me. Checking in to see what you are accepting into your mind and creating your life with is important. It's living life with awareness and intention. I continued to filter the messages, and at one point, words were spoken that I just couldn't accept and they were significant enough that it was the last time I stepped into that church, and it was the end of my practicing religion as a Catholic. It was an interesting time, and I remember initially feeling lost. If I don't go to church on Sunday, what do I do? It felt so strange and almost wrong. Almost.

As I said earlier, holidays heighten your feelings and what is going on in your life. *If I no longer go to church and no longer practice Catholicism and the birth of Christ at Christmas and Easter, then what is Christmas? What is Easter? If my beliefs have changed, then what do I do now during these holidays? If I take out the celebration of the rising of Christ, what is Easter morning other than a candy fest?* Without knowing it, a single decision to stop going to church started an avalanche of traditions and beliefs that needed to be revisited. For several years, I attempted to continue fitting into the mold I came from, and while it felt okay, it never felt great. At family gatherings, I felt as though I wasn't living "their" way, but I also wasn't living "my" way because, in truth, I didn't know what my way was. I tried different things and tried creating my own traditions, but nothing was sticking. Then I got married and noticed how, for the most part, we simply followed the family traditions versus creating what felt right for us, and that was because we didn't know what felt right for us. It was much like playing a game of cards and following suit with the hope of winning the game if you have a good enough strategy. We lacked strategy. We also lacked clarity.

Years went on, and the holidays still did not feel right because I never took the time to identify and get clear on what they meant for me. All I knew is what they weren't. At the very least, they were a time to be with family, and I could go along with that. I became somewhat satisfied getting together with family though the fuss and stress I felt around me never felt right.

When my marriage ended, the holidays had a new twist. Some say building a new house is easier than doing a renovation and maybe this holds true for traditions and how to spend the holidays. In essence, I now had a blank canvas. There was nowhere I had to be, nothing I had to do. No expectations. So, I began asking myself: *What would I like to draw on my canvas? What feels right for me? What do I want?* The answers didn't come overnight, and in truth, at the writing of this chapter, I remain unclear on what the holidays mean to me and how I desire to spend them. I can tell I'm getting closer and the reason I say that is because I am feeling better and happier during the holidays than I have in the past. If you are looking for a telltale sign, how you feel is it, and I was feeling better.

What I know for sure is I won't be dipping my paintbrush into any pail of "should" as I paint on my fresh canvas. Like any piece of art, it will take time to create. Inspiration and experiences will come over time and help to create something new. Noticing what feels right is as important as noticing what feels wrong so all experiences will bring value. At this time, what is on my canvas is the desire to not be so busy, and to be doing things that feel right both in the days and weeks prior to the holiday, and on the actual holiday. I want to be in the present moment and honor the spirit within versus the "should." This probably sounds a bit vague but I think it is perfect: notice the feelings and go with what feels right.

Easter 2014 brought clarity to much of what I just wrote about above. The day started with my daughter, marveling at the trail of candy leading from her room, down the stairs, and into the living room. Her eyes brightened even more when she spotted her Easter basket filled with candy and more. She giggled as she found candy in the craziest places, like her shoes. My mom always put candy in our shoes, and it is something I too love to do so it has become a tradition I have chosen to keep. Mid-morning, my daughter had a neighborhood friend come over for a scavenger hunt I planned for the two of them. I loved that I took the initiative to plan something that felt right for us. Having a treasure hunt in comfy clothes on Easter morning was certainly breaking tradition. No lace-trimmed dresses to grin and bear. No tight elastic around anyone's neck to hold a hat in place. Though laced trimmed dresses and hats would never be a part of our Easter even if we were heading off to church, it did bring forth the first point of reflection I had that day: how many times did I do something that didn't feel right when I was a child, teen and young adult, and how many traditions have I practiced as an adult whether or not they felt right for me?

On this day, the feeling behind the activity was notably different than in the past when I was trying to plan something to fill a void, fill the loss that I felt during the holidays. I reflected on the first Christmas we spent on our own after my separation. My daughter had just turned four. She loved playing with the train set at Chapters, so I decided to buy her one for Christmas thinking it was the perfect gift. It came with a table and what seemed like a million pieces that needed to be assembled. I had no idea when I bought it that it was the perfect gift for me as well as for her. The process of putting it together took my mind off of my current reality. It took the entire day to assemble. We fiddled and played, fiddled and played. It was a wonderful diversion because it wasn't possible to think about two things at once. It kept me in the moment, and in the moment, I was on the floor with my beautiful daughter. My mind was kept occupied with reading the instructions and assembling the pieces, both keeping me from feeling the intense grief, loss, and confusion that filled my heart.

Six and a half years later, a similar and different experience occured. Both at Christmas and at Easter my intent was to create an experience for Annika that she would enjoy. What was different this time was the feeling within me. There was no need for a diversion, or to numb the feelings within. It felt good, not painful, to be in the moment. There was no need for false laughter. Instead it came naturally. For so long I wondered if I would every authentically laugh again, and now, I am laughing and feeling joy in a more pure and truer way than I ever have. As hard as the journey has been, I find myself feeling grateful because I think without it, I would never feel the joy and contentment I do today. Processing emotions and getting in touch with your deepest self is the hardest and most rewarding work you will do in this lifetime.

This year, Annika spent Christmas with her dad. They went to her grandmother's at noon. She was gone for the rest of the day and overnight. Throughout the day I noticed how I was checking in with myself to see how I was feeling. I visualized my heart like a container that holds feelings. *What did I feel in my heart today?* In the past when it was filled with grief, I felt pain, and it is human nature to want to rid yourself of pain. Creating busyness, building a toy train set and sleeping were all ways I found to manage the pain. *What was going on today? What was happening in my heart today? Was I okay being alone?* I noticed the feeling was different from prior years. *What was different?* The answer came. There was an absence of pain in my heart. It felt okay to be alone. The anxiety, angst, and grief had lifted. I didn't feel the need to ensure I had strategies in place to manage the pain that came when grief was the main emotion in my heart. Today, I felt joy, peace, and contentment moving into my heart space. What a celebration! *When did this happen?* I wondered. Of course, it didn't just happen. It isn't something that gets turned on and off. Arriving at this place occurred because of a process that involved feeling, healing and releasing emotions. It requires awareness, developing the courage to feel the different emotions as they surface, learning how to express them in a safe and freeing way, acceptance, forgiveness, ownership, healing, learning what I wanted, and of course, time. It's a significant process and worth every painstaking moment because it frees you.

During the process, it occurred to me that some of the losses I was feeling were not necessarily losses of what I had, but rather losses of what I had hoped to have. I was grieving the loss of a dream, not the loss of a reality. It was a loss of what could be, not what was.

A loss of possibility and potential, not a loss of what existed. Whether the loss was real or that of a dream, it still hurt, it still needed to be felt and acknowledged, and there was still a knee jerk reaction at times to "do" something to numb it or make it go away, if only for the day. On the flip side, it opened the door for me to identify what I wanted and helped me realize my desires were not lost. They just weren't going to show up in the way I had thought. Looking back, I can see they weren't supposed to and learning to trust everything that is happening is happening for your higher good has been a great lesson. Trust me, I know this belief is not always easy to embrace.

I felt extreme gratitude for a heart space that was void of painful emotions in that moment. If my heart was a reservoir and in the past, it was filled with painful emotions, then in that moment it felt as though the reservoir was empty. There was no need for unnecessary busyness to numb the feelings. There were no panic-filled thoughts. I felt no need to fill the space with past traditions for the sake of filling it. On that day, in that moment, the space felt good. It felt free of pain. It felt safe. I found myself rejoicing (kind of appropriate for Easter morning, don't you think?) because for years I held onto the belief of one day feeling differently and the long-awaited day finally arrived. Many times, I felt unsure if the grief-filled feelings would ever dissolve. Today the reservoir that held my feelings appeared empty. Sometimes empty brings forth painful feelings. Today the emptiness brought joyous feelings. The feelings that come after healing. Feelings of strength, hope, and new life. It felt good for the reservoir to feel empty. I thought, *Let it be empty and clean, so I can move forward with joy in my heart, contentment, and a true knowing that the space will only stay empty if that is what I desire and choose.* Then another thought quickly came, *Perhaps it isn't empty at all right now. Maybe it's full.*

How many times do you attempt to fill a void or numb a feeling with something that only offers short-term relief? What if you allow yourself to open up during these times and allow yourself to feel what lies within versus seeking temporary relief? Could it be that in doing so you find permanent relief? Permission to let yourself be, to feel sadness, loss, anger, and anxiety is not widely accepted and encouraged in our culture. Instead, quick fixes or things that "snap you out of it" are the recommended remedies. **If you want to heal it, you need to feel it.** It's a wonderful gift to give yourself and isn't it interesting that many holidays are focused on gift giving? The gift of feeling and healing will be a gift that nourishes you infinitely, one you can pass along to future generations. Now that is a gift worth giving and receiving!

Open Your Journal

- As you read this chapter, what feelings are showing up for you?

- Is there a feeling you are denying or a fear you are afraid to acknowledge? If you are not sure, look to see if you are practicing any numbing behaviors during the holidays: overeating, working extra hours, excessive shopping, withdrawing, drinking, feeling irritable, anxious or depressed. The feeling you are denying lies underneath these actions and behaviors.

- Your inner self knows what you are feeling and why. Allow yourself to sit quietly and ask yourself what it would look and feel like if you didn't do whatever behavior(s) you identified above. Write what comes. Let it flow.

- Give yourself permission to feel your feelings. You don't have to act on everything that comes right away, but you can bring it into your awareness and begin taking a small step toward healing it and making changes that create a more honoring holiday experience.

As you have heard me say many times, it is a process, and looking back I can see the many baby steps I took along the way, and the habit I developed to notice what I was feeling within. This Easter Sunday, I noticed I was okay doing what felt right and not doing something mindlessly or for the purpose of filling the void. I was alone for the rest of the day after taking my daughter to her dad's. I would be remiss if I didn't acknowledge that I still found it difficult to allow the day to be what it needed to be. It was a day that held no past and no thoughts of what may lie ahead in the future. It was a day filled with "right now," and on a physical level there was nothing to do, nowhere to be.

In his book, *The Untethered Soul*, Michael Singer writes, *"I am learning to be the seer of my life. I am not my life."* Trust me, this takes some practice, and I guess that is why yoga and meditation are called practices. In the afternoon, I found my own yoga and meditation practice, which came in the form of washing windows. I have washed many windows over the years, but it was different this time. It was like a meditation. I washed them slowly and with awareness. I wasn't trying to keep busy or divert my thoughts and feelings. Today, washing windows served to keep me present. I noticed the kids playing outside and the wonderful sounds that came from their joy-filled bodies. I noticed families spending time together. I noticed other houses in the neighborhood were quiet, perhaps the people were gone for the day, or perhaps they had teenagers and adult children, so Easter is celebrated differently now. Perhaps they don't celebrate Easter. I noticed how the feelings came and went much like the clouds came and went in the sky. It's amazing how many thoughts and feelings passed through: joy, sadness, curiosity, contentment, fear. I noticed them all, felt them all and let them all go. I noticed I was okay in the space I was in. No desire to celebrate Easter the way my family did, even though there were many good memories attached to it. No desire to go back and be with my daughter's dad. I was content to be where I was, on my deck washing windows.

At the end of the day, I noticed how well I cared for myself throughout the day. I nourished myself with beautiful and healthy food, enjoyed a luxurious bath and beautiful lotions. I silently expressed appreciation for the body I had, the health I was enjoying, and the love and contentment I was feeling.

As I tucked into bed for the night, I noticed my heart opening. I noticed the feelings of love I had within. I realized this beautiful love was under all the feelings that needed to be felt and released. It's been there all along. It was covered up by hurt and unexpressed emotion. We hear about giving heartfelt gifts. What's in your heart? Maybe I should say, "What's on the top layers?" **For us to give a heartfelt gift in its truest form, we first need to heal our own heart. We can only give what we have.** What's in your heart space? If you allowed the feelings held in this container, as I referred to it, to surface, what would they be? The journey into your own heart and seeing, feeling and expressing what you find is your gateway to a beautiful life. You find your way out by going in.

Easter is the celebration of new life. Moving forward, Easter has a new and wonderful meaning for me. It is a time to let go of what no longer serves me (death) and plant seeds for the desires that do serve me (birth). I will teach this tradition to my daughter. I will also teach her to continue traditions that feel right for her and let go of traditions that no longer serve her. She is already much better at this than I am so like with many things, she is my teacher, she is leading the way.

Before turning the light out, I pondered how beautiful gardens grow from clean, nutrient dense soil. If my heart was the soil from which all things in my life grew, I was excited to think of how I was able to churn the soil and transform it from being filled with anger and grief to being rich with love, joy, and appreciation. Imagine the garden that can grow from such soil? Many of us have heard the saying, *"You reap what you sow,"* and while the seed is important, so too is the soil you are placing it in. Louise Hay teaches us to take wonderful thoughts into our sleep, and these are the quintessential of wonderful thoughts.

Open Your Journal

- Pick a holiday and write the traditions you currently practice or participate in.

- Notice if they are things you like to do or feel you *should* do.

- As you ponder the holiday, both the weeks leading up to it and the actual day(s), what feels right about it? What doesn't feel right?

- Look at what doesn't feel right. Why are you doing it?

- What would it feel like to not do it? If several people are involved, what changes can be made to move toward something that feels better for you?

Small changes over time create desired results. Decide to take a small step. Give thought to the change you would like to make weeks, or better yet, months before the actual holiday, so you set everyone up for success! **You can do what is right for you and still honor those around you. Be gentle. Be true**. Remember, choosing to do one thing differently, even if it seems very small and insignificant, breathes choice and empowerment into you. It is a beginning, and it will shift the energy within creating space and permission for more honoring changes.

Place 18

A Place Within The Place In Between

"A mind that is stretched by a new experience can never go back to its old dimensions."
~ Oliver Wendell Holmes Jr.

I have learned that as we heal and begin living true to our new beliefs, it is common and normal to step into new places in between. Life is a continuum of experiences, and your experiences create the fabric of your life. As mentioned in an earlier chapter, experiences are neither good nor bad, they are just experiences. Your interpretation adds meaning to them. Each and every day you have experiences, and many of them can bring new awareness to the surface and new feelings to acknowledge, feel, heal and release. I found the more I got in touch with my feelings and began understanding what they were communicating to me, the more I welcomed and honored any and all feelings that surfaced throughout my day. I began seeing them as trusted friends and embraced learning what my different feelings were attempting to communicate to me. This process resulted in increased self-compassion because instead of criticizing myself for the anger and irritation I felt, I would say, *Why are you feeling so angry right now? What are you afraid of? What are you uncertain of? What doesn't feel right? Is the anger protecting you? Who are you angry at? What do you want to say?* What a different way of speaking to myself than in the past. There was less judgment and more willingness to understand and open up to my body's wisdom. I understood that if my actions were not in alignment with my values and beliefs, my body would communicate it to me through my emotions. I became attuned with my inner wisdom and vowed I would always listen to it.

When you have done a lot of personal work, there is a tendency to think you have arrived and have it all figured out. What a lovely thought. The reality is experiences as well as learning, feeling and healing are lifelong processes. This is not meant to discourage you, but rather to bring understanding so you can act compassionately when an experience evokes a particular emotion, or whatever feeling your body uses to communicate with you when you are either off your path, living in disconnect with your values, or finding yourself entering a new place in between.

Have you arrived at a place where your buttons are being pushed again? Maybe you find yourself feeling confused or at a crossroads again. Maybe it feels as though you are standing in front of a cavern - a big hole and you need to find a pathway around it. A different way needs to be considered. Life is like this. Sometimes you can't keep going. Sometimes life stops you. Sometimes you say, "Enough!" and stop yourself. At these times, it is helpful and sometimes essential to look at things in a different way. Are you ready to own your feelings and honor them? What does it feel like as you stand at that crossroad? Are you open to looking at things differently? What feelings does the very thought of owning and / or making changes that serve you stir within? Are you ready for change or are you okay if things remain the same?

Sometimes you choose to pause. Sometimes life forces you to pause. Sometimes feeling under the weather creates the opportunity you need to pause and reflect. Honor this opportunity instead of waiting for the volume to get turned up. When an opportunity is created for you to stop, check in with your feelings and notice what is happening. How are you showing up in the world and how are you feeling about it? Are your ways similar or different from those in the past? Are you falling back into old ways or have your patterns of interaction changed to be more in line with what feels right to you? Maybe the new place in between is creating the opportunity for you to see how far you have come. Maybe it is creating the opportunity for you to implement and practice new beliefs and patterns of interaction that are more honoring. Maybe it is showing you the next piece you need to explore on your journey to living true to what feels right for you.

Open Your Journal

- What is showing up for you right now?

- How are you responding?

- Do you see old patterns slipping back in?

- Are you participating in a new way?

- How does it feel?

- What outcomes are you experiencing?

Exploration of the above questions can lead you to see that even though it might feel as though you have been in this place before, you are never in the same place. You are not the same you. Even if you have fallen back into old patterns that don't serve you, applaud yourself for how quickly you noticed it. Think about it like an onion. As you process feelings and experiences, it's like peeling off a layer of an onion. When you peel a layer from an onion, you find another layer. Though the next layer looks similar, it is not the same layer as the one you just peeled away. The same holds true in life. Although there might be similarities in a situation, it can never be exactly the same because you are not the same person and each experience will be slightly different despite its commonalities. Look for the differences. Look for the progress and build upon it.

Also remember, when you are feeling discord in one area of your life, it is common to experience similar feelings in other areas of your life because everything is connected. While it might feel disconcerting to have discord in so many areas, if all is connected then when you resolve a feeling in one area, pieces in other areas get resolved as well (see Place 12, *Pulling the Thread*). Hopefully, this thought brings reassurance that moving forward does not have to be as daunting as it appears and the rewards are so worth it.

I found it important to keep the above considerations at the forefront of my mind because it is human nature to throw your arms up in frustration and defeat if you think you have made no progress. You are not the same person. You are not in the exact same place. If all areas of your life feel like they are affected, well, in truth they are and it's okay. You are not in the same place but in the next place. Train your mind to feel excitement about the new information that is presenting. Sometimes I look at my life like it's a 1000 piece puzzle. Each experience offers another piece. Have you ever done a puzzle where 100 pieces of it are very similar? At times, it feels like you are never going to figure it out, but if you keep going and add even one small piece, it often leads you to the next piece. Life is similar. Keep stepping. Some days the steps won't feel like much. Some days they will be frustrating. Just like you look at the cover of the puzzle box for inspiration, remind yourself how you want your day to look and feel and keep that vision and those feelings in front of you.

Allow this understanding to give you both the fuel and willingness you need to move into a new place of chaos and personal growth. Believe it or not, you actually get better at moving through the process because you are developing skills, healing strategies, and most importantly, your intuition, along the way and with each experience you build upon your repertoire. Awareness comes to you more quickly, you see patterns faster, and you can process your feelings around experiences more efficiently. Your perspective will determine your willingness to venture forward, how you experience the process, and the outcome. I now see the truth in the saying, "The only thing that is constant is change." Change also brings about various degrees of chaos. Now, when change and chaos are before me, I say, "It looks like I am on the grow again!"

As new places in between arise and you see yourself on the grow again, you might wonder if the new places will be any less painful. Sometimes and sometimes not. Looking back at my own journey, every place I traveled through was necessary for me to be living the life I am today. With my goal being to live my highest life and to feel peace within, each stone needed to be overturned, so, painful or not, I was going there. It was more painful to consider what life would look like if I didn't. That said, for me, it is becoming easier because, with each new place I travel through, I use the skills I am developing with more awareness and understanding. The result is I move through it more gracefully and more quickly. Maybe it is simply a case of getting better with practice, and given the number of places in between I have traveled through, I have had significant practice!

I have learned a process that works for me, and when you think of a process, there is often an order in which things flow. When you follow the order, it is possible to move from one point to the next fluidly and without judgment. For me, the process starts with identifying the belief, ascertaining if it is truth or just a belief, then determining if it is a belief that serves me or needs to be changed. I become aware of my feelings and allow myself to feel each one and notice where I have felt this way in the past. I allow myself to feel and express the emotion and honor it. Sometimes honoring means kindly but firmly saying, "Enough." What I am saying enough to, however, varies. The fact that I can now see this link tells me my hard work has indeed made a difference and is serving to help me reach new heights in my life. It has taken time to arrive at a place where I can move more gently and compassionately through times of change. In the past, I felt like I was a bull in a china shop. I had few skills and little awareness of what I was feeling. All I knew was something was wrong. As such, I moved through the space much like someone wielding a machete—clear cutting and doing a lot of damage along the way. I might have rid myself of what didn't feel right, but it came at the expense of significant damage to my spirit and the spirit of others and sometimes permanently affecting a relationship that needed tweaking not destroying.

On more than one occasion, I left my job, home, and city for a new start with the thought that changing it all would surely bring the change I was seeking. Start over. There was one piece that came with me: Me. My beliefs and my wounds came with me, so in the absence of leaving these behind, the soil where I planted new seeds wasn't different. Just the geography was different, and geography alone couldn't create the change I desired. I wanted to feel different, and for that change, I needed to go in. I likened it to clear cutting a patch of land in order to build a new home. While in some ways it is easier, you remove trees that are beautiful and would bring such joy to your new home. When I see this happening in new land developments, I find myself wondering if it would make more sense to take the time and money necessary to hand select the trees that need to be removed. Using this as a metaphor, you are the home. The land and trees represent the life around you. It takes time to uproot the weeds. Before uprooting a weed, you need to first know what a weed is, how to identify it and why it may or may not be what you want on your property. There is much to give thought to and to learn. Ask a horticulturist. Sometimes a weed looks like a beautiful vine and yet it has the capability of choking a mature tree.

Keeping with this analogy, what happens if you pull the weed but not the root? The same weed grows and often bigger and stronger than before. You need to remove the root, and the root represents your beliefs and your wounds. Learning, cultivating, healing, growing and letting go of beliefs that no longer serve you all take time. Be patient with the process. Be patient with yourself. If you attempt to do too much at once, it is like clear cutting. It's important to take the time to learn and to be attuned to your environment. It takes time to explore why you feel as you do and how best to move forward.

It takes time to think through how your actions will affect the whole. It takes time to give thanks for what you have, how far you have come and to continue honoring the changes that are needed.

It takes time to develop and nurture self-love. It is worth whatever time it takes. For when you arrive at a place of loving yourself, you can live freely and fully, and you can give that love and opportunity to others. The love and strength you build create the fuel for the next steps you need to take. Keep going. Continue to walk on. Your steps will become gentler and be filled with grace and peace.

Open Your Journal

Let's work with the process:

- What are you feeling?

- What belief is behind the feeling?

- Is it a truth or it is a belief you picked up along the way?

- Have you experienced a similar feeling in the past? If so, describe the situation.

- Identify the beliefs that are involved.

- Do these beliefs serve you?

- If no, what belief would serve you better?

- What does it feel like to let go of the old belief?

- What does it feel like to embrace the new belief?

- Do you want to make some changes? (It's important to acknowledge and declare it.)

- If the gap between the old and new is too great and brings fear and anxiety, what is one small step you can take?

- What do you need to do to set yourself up for success? Who can you ask for support and encouragement? What books can you read? What would help you tap into your feelings and express them? Remember, to heal it, you have to both feel and express what you are feeling. An art class? Nature walk? Coffee with a friend? Beating a punching bag? What will help you get in touch with what you are feeling and then get it out?

The place in between is all about learning to love the self. At the start of this book, I asked you to look in the mirror and notice what you say to yourself. I also suggested you write it down. Go stand in front of a mirror. What are you saying to yourself now when you look in that mirror? Do you hear kinder, gentler, and more compassionate words? Do you hear words of support, appreciation, and love? Are there days when you revert back to old language? Do you notice it happening, and then lovingly correct yourself? Make it your goal to put all language that doesn't serve you curbside for garbage pick-up. As you know, what is picked up by the garbage man is gone forever! Put it in the garbage bin, not the recycling bin. Let it go.

My hope for all of you is that the love you develop for yourself fills your heart to overflowing. I believe this can be achieved when you learn to tap into and honor your intuition and when you take steps toward honoring what feels right for you. With practice, it becomes easier and hopefully becomes your new way of existing. Couple this practice with a new perspective on your experiences. They do not define you. They have no bearing on your worthiness or whether or not you are lovable. They do not determine your future. They provide great information. In his book, *The Surrender Experiment,* Michael Singer writes that *"You are not the voice of the mind, you are the one who hears it, and you are not your experiences but the one who sees them."* Your experiences may bring to the forefront new things for you to ponder. They create the opportunity for you to see what you are holding onto, what needs healing, what needs to be acknowledged, felt, and expressed so you can let go. Notice and celebrate how far you have come and welcome the next experience and the awareness it brings.

Your life consists of many steps, and each step has value. Previous experiences and your reaction to them have led you to where you find yourself today. You will have new experiences and based on your reactions today, they will lead you to the next place. If you have been doing the journal exercises in this book, your reactions to life experiences today are likely different than they were years prior. Picture standing before a large mud-filled puddle. You might stand there for hours trying to figure out how to get over it. You may even give thought to the possibility of another route. A variety of emotions might surface at the thought of what will happen if you don't leap hard enough and land safely on the other side. How is the experience different when there are stones leading across the puddle to dry ground? All you have to focus on is placing your foot on the first one, then the next one. It becomes manageable.

Achieving the life you desire is similar. If the leap is too big, it can lead to inaction. You spend much time and energy pondering the "what-ifs" or convincing yourself where you are is okay, sometimes for years or maybe even decades. There is no shortcut, and you can't skip over it. There is a great children's song called, *Going on a Bear Hunt,* and it says it perfectly: *"Can't go over it. Can't go under it. Can't go around it. Got to go through it!"* In truth, the shortcut is to go through it with stepping stones also known as baby steps. Some people spend their entire lives trying to get over it, under it, or around it only to find out there is no way of dodging it. You have got to go through it. Why not commit to that process now so you can get to the place you desire to be instead of spending your life trying to get there? See the gift in your experiences and how they offer the stepping stones you need.

Open Your Journal

Take some time to reflect on your progress.

- How does your life currently look and feel?

- How is your life different from the way it was at the beginning of this book? Identify even the smallest of ways that it is different. Small changes done consistently lead to big changes over time.

- Do you handle situations differently than you once did?

- Have you developed the skill of saying no to what doesn't feel right and yes to what does?

- Are you more connected with your intuition?

- Are there new people in your life?

If you recall, in Place 3, *Chaos*, I talked about the chaos you are likely to experience when you step into the place in between. As you journey through it and enter experiences with new beliefs, more self-awareness, and self-love, make it a practice to notice your feelings.

Notice if you are feeling lighter, calmer, or scared. Notice if it feels good and safe to show up in a way that feels right for you. Maybe there is still some uneasiness or uncertainty. Notice if your confidence has built to the level where you are okay stepping into new places of chaos. Or, does fear supersede your confidence and you notice yourself withdrawing? Notice if you withdraw or if you return to what is comfortable. Know that these are two different places. To withdraw but not fall back into old patterns is progress. Withdrawing can be an act of self-love when the intention is to pro-tect the space you are in. Be sure to acknowledge and celebrate this big step. Maybe you find yourself vacillating between wanting to step into a new place and wanting to hold back. Notice the messages you are getting from your head and the ones that are coming from your body. Can you tell what messages are coming from your head (old beliefs, aka gremlins) and which messages are coming from your soul, your heart, your gut...the deepest part of you? Notice the feelings, feel them and be open to the messages they bring. Allow your feelings to be expressed. Maybe expression is verbal and is a conversation you have with someone, or maybe expression comes in the form of screaming into a pillow or some other physical action that serves to release the emotion in a safe way.

In Place 10, *Why Do We Numb Ourselves?* I mentioned several forms of expression. Allow your feelings to be acknowledged, honored and expressed. They are the gateway to the wounds that need healing, and when they are fully felt and expressed, they can be healed. As painful as this process may be, what you have been holding onto can finally be released revealing your deepest essence. You begin to see you, your gifts and your truth. Keep walking. Keep living. Keep feeling. Keep releasing. There is a treasure buried deep within that awaits you.

Moving through the place in between doesn't follow a specific template or timeline. Your experience will be as unique as you are. Avoid judging it or thinking it should go faster or slower or this way or that way. There is no right way. The experience you are having is as it needs to be. Maybe you choose to meander at different places along the way, maybe you revisit a place or two. It doesn't matter. It's simply part of your journey. **There is no right or wrong way. Be gentle with yourself. Be kind. Embrace the day and the space you are in and what comes to you in that day. All have value. Everything is happening in the perfect way and at the perfect time for you.**

Hold onto who you have become, and continue walking on in that light. Keep the life you desire in your vision and write and rewrite affirmations to support those desires. Visualizations and affirmations help you gain clarity on what you want your days to look and feel like. Be sure to include the affirmations: *I am worthy and deserving. It is safe to be me. I love and accept myself. Thank you for the strength and belief I need to carry on* because, with each step you take, you will require a new level of worthiness, safety, strength, and acceptance. Make it a daily practice to feed your mind. When your body holds these words as truths, the Universe will bring you what you need to make it a reality. Be open, be receptive, say yes and be gracious. You are worthy and deserving!

My wish for all of you is that you have the courage to step in and walk on. Walk on to a place where you can live your highest life, live the true essence of who you are, learn to embrace and feel all feelings fully, fulfill your calling and live in truth and peace. All of this is a process. It isn't a destination, and it is not about arriving. **This is your life, and it is a life worth living well. You are worthy and deserving. Everyone, including you, benefits when you strive to become the best version of yourself!**

Final Thoughts

"Success in a woman's life is not the result of a specific brand of education.
It is most often the result of a soul that has become inspired, a heart that was
ready to believe, a mind ready to grasp a vision of what is possible, and a body
that is eager to take flight."
~ Stacy James

For me, and perhaps for those reading this book, the place in between has become a treasured place. It grants me the space I need to
pause, reflect, feel, heal, replenish and rebuild. These processes are
of such value because they bring awareness and compassion, two
important ingredients for the development of the courage, strength,
and faith I needed to go forward into my world in a new and more
honoring way. The ripple effect of learning to live in a way that feels
right for me is I can accept and honor others and their choices. This
doesn't mean I have to agree. I feel no need to change them, and no
need for them to see things as I see them. When I say "yes" to being
me, I can also say "yes" to others being who they desire and/or need
to be whether it aligns with me or not. Sometimes it leads to spending more time with people, and sometimes it leads to spending less
time together, and it is all okay.

As you become more clear on who you are and how you want
to show up in this world, what people say to you has little effect,
whether they are offering a compliment or casting a judgment. You

know who and what you are and where you are going. What others think, say, or feel is simply information for you. As I've mentioned, I believe when someone says something, it tells me where they are at. How I respond tells me where I am at. If someone says something to me and it pushes a button, there is great value in exploring why it caused a reaction. Is there any truth in the comment? Is there something I can learn? Maybe it highlights something I desire to change about myself. Is it linking me to something that happened in my past and creating the opening for healing? **Be grateful for the information that comes to you. Choose what you want to accept. Own what is yours to own. Let go of the rest.**

Think about the words you speak. What is your intent when you speak? Do you feel the need to be heard? Do you feel the need to be right? Are you capable of listening, and more importantly, hearing? There is a difference. Can you communicate in a way that honors all people in the conversation including you? If someone can't understand your feelings and perspective, how do you handle that? Can you be okay with them not understanding? I've learned if what I feel comes from my heart, I feel no need to justify my feelings. When it comes from my head, I notice a need to explain and gain a person's understanding and acceptance of my thoughts and feelings. This has become a tool I use to quickly notice whether my thoughts are coming from my *heart* or my *head*? What is your intention? What is your need during conversations? How do you feel in your heart after a conversation?

When you are living your purpose, and on purpose, it won't matter what anyone else is doing, thinking or feeling. You will feel excitement for their accomplishments and their goals, dreams, and projects. You will be accepting of their choices even when they are different from yours. There still might be the tendency to question if you *should* be doing what they are doing or feeling as they feel, and these thoughts and feelings will leave as fast as they arrive when your inner knowing is strong, and you see the word "should" is at play. There are no two human beings who are the same. Even identical twins have their differences. This means that each one of us has been given unique gifts that we are to use to serve in this world. Along the way, these gifts got buried, and by stepping into the place in between and walking on, you are saying yes to uncovering your unique gifts, yes to healing past wounds, yes to living fully and in truth.

The place in between principles can be applied to any place in your life where the beliefs you have adopted as truths no longer serve you. And in order to move forward, you need to bring awareness to the beliefs you hold as truths and let go of them and embrace new ones.

The experiences you have are linked to the beliefs you hold. Beliefs create your thoughts, which then create your actions, and in turn, create your life. Since a belief is not necessarily a truth unless you deem it to be, then it can be said that everything in life is made up and therefore everything in life can be changed. If something doesn't feel right or if you are living in a way that no longer serves you, the script is not etched in stone. You have the ability to change how you are living. Changing your beliefs and how you live is a process, one that requires exploring, acknowledging, feeling, healing, forgiveness of self and others, letting go, embracing, practicing and most of all self-love. The process will be unique for each individual. What is the same for everyone is it requires a readiness and the courage to step into the place in between. You create the life you desire by choosing the beliefs that support and serve that which you desire. The first step is acknowledging that something doesn't feel right and then opening up to what that is and why it is. This book takes you on a journey to yourself, one that is infinite.

Be kind and gentle with yourself. Know that you are always doing the best you can in any given moment with the knowledge and awareness that you have. Creating the life you desire happens one step at a time.
Step in, walk on, and then step in again and walk on. Your life depends on it.

*"Happiness occurs when how we think, feel, and act
are in alignment."*
~ Gandhi

Acknowledgments

To Louise Hay, you have been a mentor to me for decades and I am where I am today because of your teachings. I will always remember and hold close to my heart the words you spoke to me when I met you in person. Thank you.

To Jen Davis, thank you for teaching me the concept of holding the space for people as well as what it means to shine the light. These concepts have so much value.

To Michael Fischer, thank you for your big smile and introducing me to a perspective on depression that was fascinating and changed everything.

To Patrice Butts, thank you for your tremendous support during a very difficult transition. I remember with appreciation many conversations, your willingness to listen, pushing me when I needed to be pushed, and sharing words that I hold onto to this day. Heartfelt thanks to both you and my brother, Peter Anstett, for opening your home and hearts to me.

To Ellen Abernethy, Colleen Marana, and Marina Schmidt, the three of you are extraordinary practitioners, each with a very specialized and unique practice that made healing at a deep level possible. I am forever grateful for each of you and your gifts.

To Tara Kachroo and Lisbeth Lippert, I am grateful to have found two exceptional yogis. Yoga and meditation have given me much needed nourishment and help me quiet the chatter and live with awareness.

To Candace Loughran, you are the reason this book came to be. Each time we conversed, you would say, "You should write a book." Without either of us knowing it, you were planting a seed within me, and watering it each time we spoke. I finally saw the book you saw and with that, a journey began that has spanned several years and has given rise to this book. Thank you.

To Ky-Lee Hanson and Tania Moraes-Vaz, thank you for working so hard to bring this book to fruition. You have been beyond patient with this first time author. Thank you for your understanding, for keeping the ball rolling, maintaining the focus, and for your expertise. I have tremendous respect for each of you and for the work you do.

To Wendy McIssaac, fate has an interesting way of bringing people together and it did it twice with us. I admire your passion for writing and editing, and was so grateful for your willingness to share your gifts with me.

To Wendy Baetz, thank you for showing me how to live well through simplicity, awareness, and intention. Your support and encouragement are greatly appreciated.

To Heather Clarke, thank you for creating a safe place for me to explore my thoughts and express my feelings, and for offering very wise words when I need to hear them.

To Paula Renon and Frank Dingethal, thank you for your caring hearts, encouragement, and friendship. To Monika Stegmann, thank you for your support and for believing in me. I was able to take several life changing steps because of you. Saying thank you doesn't seem to be enough.

To Cory Farago and Mary Lyn Payerl, between the two of you, I have been blessed with over 80 years of friendship. Thank you for seeing me through many seasons, always with kind and unconditional hearts.

To Dianne Szymanski, thank you for being by my side during some very difficult times and for many, often daily, conversations.

To Bethany Kovarik, thank you for understanding me in a way few do.

To my Arbonne sisters, you are an inspiring group of women who have contributed to my life in immeasurable ways, both personally and professionally. From the bottom of my heart, thank you.

To my family, Mary-Lou and Donny Lang, Jules and Jamie Kovarik, Peter Anstett and Patrice Butts, and my nieces and nephews, each of you have contributed to my life and where I am today in a special and unique way. I am grateful for each one of you. Special thanks to Donny Lang for helping me on so many occasions. As Annika says, "You really can fix anything."

To my late Mom and Dad, I feel your presence and support in the most wonderful ways and will be forever grateful for all you gave to me, did for me, and taught me. I miss you both.

To my daughter, Annika, Kahlil Gibran says, "You may house their bodies but not their souls." I love watching you unfold. I feel blessed that our souls are together in this lifetime. May we love, accept, hear, see and support each other as we journey through life. I love you to the moon and back.

To Jasper, I am beyond grateful for a soul that not only held the space for me, but also sat in it with me until I was strong enough to be on my own. You will always have a special place in my heart.

References

1. Altucher, J. and Altucher, C.A. 2014. *"The Power of No."* United States: Hay House Inc.

2. Canfield, Jack. 2005. *"The Success Principles."* New York, NY: Harper Collins

3. Carson, R. 2003. *"Taming Your Gremlin."* New York, NY: Harper Collins.

4. Hay, L. 1991. *"The Power is Within You."* United States: Hay House Inc.

5. Hay, L. 1997. *"Empowering Women."* United States: Hay House Inc.

6. Hay, L. 1999. *"You Can Heal Your Life."* United States: Hay House Inc.

7. Hay, L. and Holden, R. 2015 *"Life Loves You."* United States: Hay House Inc.

8. Hay, L. and Kessler, D. 2014. *"You Can Heal Your Heart."* United States: Hay House Inc.

9. Hay, L. and Richardson, C. 2011. *"You Can Create An Exceptional Life."* United States: Hay House Inc.

10. Jacobs, L. 2017. *"Beautiful Money."* New York, NY: Penguin Random House.

11. Northrup, K. 2013. *"Money: A Love Story."* United States: Hay House Inc.

12. Olson, J. 2005. *"The Slight Edge."* Lake Dallas, Texas: Success Books.

13. Ruiz, D. M. 1997. *"The Four Agreements."* San Rafael, California: Amber-Allen Publishing Inc

Paula Anstett is a seeker of understanding. She challenges the status quo on a daily basis by constantly asking "why?" Determined for her choices to not only make sense but to also feel right, Paula was constantly in search of information to help her navigate her internal conflict.

It took, what she refers to as a train crash in her life, for her to realize that she was searching in the wrong place. The answers weren't out there—they were within her. And so, the journey from her head to her heart began. This was a journey that required awakening her intuition—the place deep within that held the answers to all her questions; answers that would finally feel right.

Paula has been on a lifelong adventure involving change, learning, growth, and healing. A graduate of the University of Waterloo and the Institute of Holistic Nutrition, she says that while she has learned and acquired great information in the classroom, she gained immense knowledge in life's own classroom.She lives in Waterloo, Ontario with her greatest teacher, her daughter Annika. Connect with Paula at www.paulaanstett.com to learn more about her work and offerings.

Golden Brick Road
Publishing House

Locking arms and helping each other down their Golden Brick Road

At Golden Brick Road Publishing House, we lock arms with ambitious people and create success through a collaborative, supportive, and accountable environment. We are a boutique shop that caters to all stages of business around a book. We encourage women empowerment, and gender and cultural equality by publishing single author works from around the world, and creating in-house collaborative author projects for emerging and seasoned authors to join.

Our authors have a safe space to grow and diversify themselves within the genres of poetry, health, sociology, women's studies, business, and personal development. We help those who are natural born leaders, step out and shine! Even if they do not yet fully see it for themselves. We believe in empowering each individual who will then go and inspire an entire community. Our Director, Ky-Lee Hanson, calls this: *The Inspiration Trickle Effect.*

If you want to be a public figure that is focused on helping people and providing value, but you do not want to embark on the journey alone, then we are the community for you.

To inquire about our collaborative writing opportunities or to bring your own idea into vision, reach out to us at www.goldenbrickroad.pub

Goals, Brilliance, and Reinvention

Join us at the social

www.gbrsociety.com

GBR Society is a community of authors, future authors, readers, and supporters. We are connected through Golden Brick Road Publishing House; a leadership, empowerment, and self-awareness publisher. The GBR empire is built on sharing opportunity. It is a brand built on being a true community consisting of friendship, allies, support, advancing with each other, philanthropy, and tribe work. We struggle together and we flourish together. We are a community budding with endless ongoing love. Get to know the real people behind successful author brands and careers. Build friendships with motivated people and find your own voice. We have been said to be guides in helping others discover their own strength.

Join us as a reader and gain a wealth of insight from our authors and featured guests, while receiving access to exclusive advanced books, online and in person events, bookclubs, summits, online programs, retreats, and special offers. Learn from us how to advance in your personal and professional life. Access information on what interests you, choosing from health and wellness, sociology, human rights, writing and reading, creating a business, advancing a business or career, and personal development including self-esteem, introspection, self-discovery, and self-awareness.

Notes

Notes

Notes

Notes

Notes